LOVE THAT LASTS

LOVE THAT LASTS

How to help your relationship
survive and grow

Bill & Lynne Hybels

Marshall Pickering
An Imprint of HarperCollins*Publishers*

Marshall Pickering is an Imprint of
HarperCollins*Religious*
Part of HarperCollins*Publishers*
77–85 Fulham Palace Road, London w6 8jb

First published in Great Britain in 1995 by Marshall Pickering
as part of the title *Making Love Last*

This revised edition 1999

1 3 5 7 9 10 8 6 4 2

© 1991 Bill and Lynne Hybels

Bill and Lynne Hybels assert the moral right to be
identified as the authors of this work.

A catalogue record for this book is
available from the British Library.

ISBN 0 551 03181 6

Printed and bound in Great Britain by
Caledonian International Book Manufacturing Ltd, Glasgow

All scripture quotations, unless otherwise noted,
are taken from the *Holy Bible: New International Version*
(North American Edition). Copyright © 1973, 1978, 1984
by the International Bible Society. Used by permission of
Zondervan Bible Publishers.

CONDITIONS OF SALE

To Mr and Mrs K. K. Gregory,
for their remarkable friendship.
And to the staff and congregation of
Willow Creek Community Church,
for allowing us to minister
in the midst of our humanness.

Contents

Acknowledgments

When we signed the contract to write this book, we thought we were allowing ourselves ample time to complete the manuscript. Then came real life. One thing after the next interfered with our writing, and we became hopelessly behind schedule. We owe many thanks to Zondervan's Jim Buick, Scott Bolinder, and John Sloan. Jim and Scott watched more than one deadline pass unmet, and responded with grace. John again proved to be an insightful and patient editor; knowing how critical the editor/author relationship is, we thank God for him. During all our dealings with Zondervan, we felt like we were among friends.

Frequently during the writing process, we found it necessary to run away to a quiet place where we could think, talk, and work uninterrupted. Bob and Linda Buford, Rich and Helen DeVos, Jack and Clara Mains, and Ed and Elsa Prince generously provided beautiful places for us to run to. Grandma and Grandpa Barry and Greg and Corinne Ferguson lovingly covered the home front while we were away. Buster helped, too.

Jim Dethmer, Greg and Corrine Ferguson, and Russ Robinson helped tremendously by reading the manuscript and offering both encouragement and constructive criticism. This book is better for their careful attention to detail.

In recent months we've written many things about our marriage. Let us add just one more: Our marriage has produced two great kids. Each night when we tucked Todd into bed he prayed that 'Mum and Dad would do a good job on the book'. And Shauna's probing questions about what it was 'really like' when we were dating brought to mind many memories that found their way onto the following pages.

Roller Coaster Romance

'You're driving too fast for road conditions.'
'I've got it under control.'

Our voices cut sharply above the speeding click of the windshield wipers.

For hours the sleet had pounded the windshield. For hours we had sat in bitter silence.

Thank God for the darkness. Thank God the kids slept quietly in the back of our blue and grey Suburban. Thank God we were almost home.

It should have been a wonderful Christmas vacation. Our Washington DC accommodations, reserved and paid for by a generous friend, were comfortable and roomy. The kids, feeling very grown-up at eleven (Shauna) and eight (Todd), enjoyed the freedom to roam alone through the huge old hotel which was nearly deserted because of the holidays; they were delighted to let Mum and Dad sleep in while they went downstairs to order breakfast on their own. Our tourist schedule was relaxed and modified to meet the kids' desires: their ideal afternoon balanced two hours at the Smithsonian with two hours in the hotel pool. Historic Georgetown was within walking distance, and each evening we strolled by the windows of quaint shops and chose from an assortment of curious eateries. One evening, while the boys 'cruised' the town, the girls laughed and cried through Dickens' *A Christmas Carol* at the Ford Theatre. Sounds wonderful, doesn't it?

For the kids it was – we hope; we did our best to create a memorable experience for them. But for us it was a dreadful week. Pleasant accommodations and a carefully planned itinerary could not ease the pain of our troubled marriage. The inviting king-sized bed in our private room could not bridge the gap between estrangement and intimacy. Frustration, loneliness, hopelessness, fear, despair, grief – they overshadowed every potential joy and defied every attempt to break through them. While the kids roamed we talked, but every conversation drove us further apart. We became increasingly dissatisfied with ourselves and angry at one another. We felt trapped, as we had so often in the past. Our commitments to the children, to the church, and to God kept us clinging to a marriage that all too often broke our hearts.

We drove into our driveway on the first day of the new year.

Happy New Year.

———

'I've never seen so many stars.'

'It's like a black velvet dome studded with diamonds.'

Lazy waves eased slowly up the sandy beach, then rolled back in the dark ocean waters. We lay on our backs on the sand, dreamy from the hypnotic rhythm of the gentle seas. There was not a hint of chill in the night air. Ah, to be cradled in creation.

The only thing that matched the perfection of that night was the day that had preceded it. We had awakened to a drizzly dawn, sipped lemon tea in our tiny rented cottage, then walked the beach towards the rainbow that arched in the south. The colours brightened while we watched, then faded as the morning sun sucked the moisture from the air. We walked waist deep in the water, then dove beneath the shimmering surface. We swam till our muscles ached, then let the buoyant swells carry us back towards shore. Tiny, silver slips of fish skimmed the surface of the water beside us, then flashed and dove and chased in an underwater playground of conches and clams and moon shells. Refreshed by our swim, we showered the salt from our hair, then dressed for the day in appropriate vacation attire – another swimsuit. We ate a late breakfast of granola and fruit, then each grabbed a book, scrunched sand and beach towels into chairlike moulds, and aimed our sunscreened faces towards the south.

The weather, with its cloudless sky, was at its best; and more importantly, we were at our best. The days of unrushed living had softened our rough edges and mellowed our intensities. We spoke softly and laughed easily. We traded books back and forth, insisting that the other read the 'wonderful passages' we had just read. We compared notes and insights. We reminisced and talked of the future. We revealed fears and acknowledged foibles and discussed dreams and shared secrets.

And the pleasure of that day gave way to romance beneath the stars.

Despair in the front seat of a Chevy Suburban? Or romance under a diamond sky? Which describes the real Hybels' marriage?

They both do. In fact, those two real-life episodes occurred within months of one another. It hardly seems possible, yet bounding between those dramatic contrasts has been the pattern of our relationship since we met at seventeen. Our highs have been heart-throbbingly wonderful; our lows have been devastating. During the highs we think that meeting one another was the best thing that ever happened to us; during the lows we rue the day our paths crossed.

───────────

Let us tell you how it all began...

Spring, 1969. J & D Roller Rink, Portage, Michigan. Ladies' Choice.

She watches him as she had done at several other Youth for Christ activities. He is blond and blue-eyed and handsome, with an air of confidence that intrigues her. She wonders if he has noticed her.

He has. And he is curious about the person behind the title of Michigan's Junior Miss. While she ponders whether or not to ask him to skate, he steals a quick glance at her, hoping she will ask.

She does, and it is not the only skate they share that evening. When the party ends they go their separate ways, but they have, without a doubt, 'connected'.

'Hey, Mum, I met this guy, Bill Hybels. I really like him. I hope I see him again.'

Bill offers no similar comment to his mother, but he fully intends to see Lynne Barry again – soon.

Just days later, in a church parking lot in Kalamazoo, a group of high schoolers gathers to carpool to a YFC retreat at Spring Arbor College. Car assignments are made, and by some mysterious gift of fate, *she* ends up in the front seat of *his* car.

A country music fan, he tunes his radio to *Alabama*'s nasal twang. A classical flautist, she chides him for his down-home taste. They laugh at their little difference, and talk nonstop for the next two hours, oblivious to their back-seat riders.

The weekend schedule sends them both into musical competition – she in a flute trio, he in a small band where he sings and plays guitar and string bass. There is plenty of free time, however, and they use it well – quiet conversations in the deserted student lounge, long walks on country roads, an 'against the rules' drive to a nearby town. They seem to have so much in common: they both love water sports – swimming, skiing, and especially sailing. And their fathers both fly aeroplanes and drive motorcycles. She hangs on every word while he tells of sailing across Lake Michigan in a furious rainstorm. He laughs at her comic adventure of learning to drive a motorbike – and crashing into a garbage can.

They talk, too, of more significant things: their shared faith, their commitment to ministry, their college plans, their values, their appreciation of their respective families. There seems to be so much potential in this relationship – and not *just* because they have a lot in common. There is something else, too.

It manifests itself in the laughter that punctuates every conversation, in the fun that surrounds every encounter, in the warmth that envelopes the entire weekend. There is a spark between them. There is magic. There is chemistry.

Too soon the weekend ends. But the next evening he calls her. She is teaching a private flute lesson, so she asks him to call again. By the time he calls back, she is being visited by another young man she has been dating, so she asks him to try again later. Angry at being put off, he decides to call one more time. If she refuses to take *this* call…

She doesn't. They plan their first official date.

It is Friday evening and they drive west on M-43 towards South Haven. a little resort town on the eastern shore of Lake Michigan. On the way they stop at an auction, for no particular reason except perhaps to hear the country music blasting from crude loudspeakers attached to the front of the dilapidated warehouse. Back in the car, they continue to the lake, park at South Beach, and walk barefoot across the sand and onto the pier. They sit beneath the red lighthouse that flashes its warning and watch the parade of boats that glide between the two concrete breakwaters to moor for the night. In the distant west, sails make sharp silhouettes against the pink and purple sunset.

While they sit and talk, a cool breeze drifts in. They scoot closer together to fend off the chill, grateful for an excuse to break through the reserve that separates them. Because of the fun of the previous weekend, this evening does not hold the normal discomforts of a first date. Still, there are the inevitable questions. *Is* she *having a good time? Is* he *having a good time? Should I hold her hand? Why doesn't he hold my hand?*

The truth is, they are both having a good time, and though she is somewhat disappointed when he does not request a goodnight kiss, they both know they will be seeing much more of one another.

They date steadily throughout the summer. Twice a week, at least, he arrives at her house in the pickup trick he drives when he works on the farms owned by his father's produce company. It is a demanding summer job – long hours in hot, dusty, backbreaking conditions. But he has worked hard for his dad since he was five, and he takes it in his stride. She is impressed with his sense of responsibility and his devotion to hard work and discipline. He is capable and motivated and goal oriented, and she respects that.

For him the dates are no small thing. It is not uncommon for him to work from sunup to past sundown; on the days they plan to meet he has to work extra hard to be able to leave before dark. It is an hour's drive from the farm to her house, and even before he starts the drive he is exhausted. Often he arrives at her house sweaty and caked with dust, straight from the fields, and she rides with him to his parents' home where he showers and dresses for the evening. Picking her up before he goes home saves a little time, and every extra moment counts. There is something about this girl that makes him want to grasp every possible moment to be with her. He appreciates her intelligence and depth, her gentleness and sensitivity.

What draws them together perhaps more than anything else is that they see one another as true peers. Neither feels 'in charge' of their relationship. There is a mutuality of respect and appreciation that places them on an equal footing, and sets this relationship apart from any that either of them had known in the past.

By the end of summer they know this is a serious relationship. Unfortunately, in September she leaves for Wheaton College near Chicago; he stays in Kalamazoo to finish his last year of high school. The relationship turns into a series of anxious trips to the mailbox, late-night phone calls, and weekend visits, a pattern which continues for the next five years. Well, it doesn't exactly continue. In reality, it starts and stops – and starts again – repeatedly throughout those years. They are voluntary victims of a quintessential on-and-off again romance, complete with a broken engagement and a year and a half of total separation.

I don't have to put up with this grief, she thinks, as she throws out his letters and shoves his graduation picture into a padded mailer.

I can be happier with someone else, he mumbles, as he fingers through the directory of women students at Dordt College in Sioux Center, Iowa.

But she cannot forget the wonderful moments that *hadn't* been touched by grief. And he finds out that he *isn't* happier with someone else.

So they try again, and find that they have grown during eighteen months apart. As individuals they are more mature, and that maturity translates into a more stable and satisfying relationship. They are married on 18 May 1974.

It is grand occasion with all the usual trappings – and then some. By now, the twenty-two-year-old groom is the pastor of a growing youth ministry, and the 'kids' seem to have taken over the wedding. With their youthful exuberance they have lent a kind of carnival atmosphere to a typically formal affair. Impatiently the bride and groom greet guests at the reception, anxious to leave the carnival behind and head for a Florida honeymoon.

They should have lingered at the carnival wedding; the honeymoon has a far less festive tone. They blame their irritability, their frequent arguments, and their emotional distance on their painfully sunburned bodies, but the real problem is their inability to resolve conflict.

A few months later they take a camping trip in upper Michigan and have a marvellous time. They huddle together under waterfalls in the Tahquamenon River. They charge through the north woods on motorbikes. They hike along the sandy shores of Lake Superior. They call it their 'real honeymoon' and forget their debacle in Florida. They see sunny days ahead.

But the storm clouds are rolling in again. The young husband's work proves to be a whirlwind that swirls faster and faster and sweeps away whatever gets in the way – like carefree walks on country roads, like leisurely breakfast conversations, like Friday night dates … like marriage.

So there are hurts and hostilities. There are sullen silences and angry outbursts. There are tears and fears and ultimatums.

And then, finally, there is brokenness. There are apologies and declarations of better intentions. There is hope. There is romance. There is, once again, a blissful string of highs.

To be followed by a new series of lows. It is not just the career demands that drive them into downward spirals. Over the years their differences have become pronounced and irritating. Oh, they still share their common values: they still bow before the same God and aim for the same life goals. But how differently they see the world. How differently they relate to other people. How differently they view marriage and family life. How differently they approach conflict. How differently they express love.

And how they misunderstand and judge one another. He feels like she is trying to reshape him to make him more acceptable to her. She feels like she has to be something she isn't in order to win his approval. They both despair of ever feeling consistently loved and accepted.

And so the story goes. From high to low to high to low again. Peaks and valleys connected by plateaus of longing and fear: longing for the next high, fear of the next low.

———

Writing of our marriage from a third-person perspective is more than a literary device. It is an attempt to gain insight into our marriage by standing outside it and looking at it objectively. For years we were mystified by the volatile nature of our relationship. Why were we so drawn to one another during that dusty summer of 1969? And why, with so many difficulties in our relationship, did we always decide to try again, even before the commitment of marriage held us together? On the other hand, why does our relationship spiral downward so easily? Why do we get so frustrated and so frequently reach painful impasses? If we love each other so much, why have we hurt each other so often?

Many hours of thinking, praying, and talking over these issues have taken some of the mystery out of those questions.

We see now that we have been drawn together by some very strong compatibilities, but then almost simultaneously shoved apart by some very strong *in*compatibilities.

Fortunately, our areas of compatibility are of the absolutely essential kind – beliefs, goals, values, and character qualities related to the very essence of who we are as individuals – commonalities without which no relationship can thrive. The *plus* in our marriage is that, when all is said and done, we chose well. We each picked a life partner we could respect and relate to as an equal.

In the beginning these areas of compatibility were so obvious and heartwarming that we weren't even aware of the many incompatibilities that lurked beneath the surface. Fortunately, the incompatibilities were of a secondary nature – temperament differences and conflicting expectations – that could be negotiated and compromised and worked through. The problem was, we did not do that. We did not use our courtship as a time to ferret out our differences and come up with plans for dealing with them. We did not learn, until recent years, how to confront conflicts without wiping each other out in the process. The *minus* in our marriage was that we let a myriad of lesser incompatibilities nip away at our relationship day in and day out.

In addition, we each sabotaged the already challenging task of marriage-building by contributing our respective boatloads of personal sins and weaknesses – which ranged from workaholism to insecurity to distorted thinking to poor communication skills to misunderstandings of true spirituality. We eventually learned that an important piece in the marriage puzzle is to get our own lives in order, so we can be whole and healthy people. Anything that diminishes us as individuals diminishes the potential of our marriage. We both had to face a lot of internal ugliness and make radical changes in how we lived in order to become 'fit' marriage partners. Years of fast pace and high pressure had made us both pretty awful people to live with.

Marriage is a humbling journey.

We want to help married people stay married. We'll offer a two-pronged plan that includes: first, working through the lesser incompatibilities that interfere with peace and mutual satisfaction, and second, learning healthy patterns of living and relating on a daily basis.

At times it will be important for one or the other of us to tell a story or give our own particular viewpoint on some issue. So as not to confuse the reader, we have used the initials of our first names in the margin to indicate who is writing.

We are not experts on marriage. If anything qualifies us for writing this book, it is that we have suffered in our marriage. We have wished on more than one occasion that we could get out of our marriage. We have wondered how God let us make such a terrible mistake. We have felt hopeless and trapped.

And, in fact, we were trapped – by our own deeply held commitments. So we did the only thing that seemed right fort us to do. We worked at it. And worked. And worked some more.

And we continue to work. Our union is still marked by high highs and low lows and probably will for as long as we live. However, the highs are becoming more enjoyable and more frequent, and the lows are becoming less devastating and less frequent. And the thread of days and months upon which these contrasting moments hang is growing stronger all the time, reinforced again and again by memories and experiences that are increasingly pleasant and peace-filled and satisfying.

Resolving Temperament Tensions

It was charming, quaint, cosy – a limestone cottage flanked by giant evergreens. Sunlight sneaked between the graceful branches, filtered through the sheer curtains, and bounced off the golden walls of the peaceful sitting room. A woman read quietly in an easy chair, a brown-eyed spaniel at her feet, while her husband busied himself with pleasant domestic chores. The young couple, newlyweds, had created in their humble abode a refuge from life's storms and had welcomed into their hearts and home two young men with no other home to claim; the four lived together in joy and harmony. When the afternoon sun began to fade the woman moved cheerily to her small but well-provisioned kitchen and prepared a feast to delight her grateful companions. Round the bountifully laden table they gathered, and the young husband offered a simple but heartfelt prayer. There hovered an aura of love.

That's the way it was, all right – in our dreams. In reality, the years we spent in our first home were anything but the fairy-tale just described. The only thing quaint about our tan brick house was its size: it was downright miniscule. The lot upon which it perched was so narrow we didn't even have room for a driveway. And the evergreens didn't flank it; they overran it. There was no way the sunlight could have sneaked between the tangle of unkempt greenery that shrouded our uncurtained windows. The golden glow that filled the living room was nothing more than the gaudy glimmer of our high-gloss canary yellow walls. The woman of the house never had time to read, and her husband avoided domestic chores at all costs. The brown-eyed spaniel? Yes, he was there, as were a black-eyed littermate and two other large dogs. The two springer spaniels were ours; the German shepherd and the Doberman belonged to our two long-term boarders. These young men may have been looking for a refuge from life's storms, but they sure didn't find it in our home. The walls of our tiny cracker box groaned against the cumulative force of four busy adults and four active dogs. Chaos, not joyful harmony, reigned. Nor did we enjoy many sumptuous meals. There was not a decent cook among us, and even when we combined our meagre earnings we could barely afford the simplest food. And the loving atmosphere? It left the house shortly after we moved in.

It was in that house, in fact, that we first began to suspect that perhaps our marriage had been a mistake. An observer might have blamed our marital frustrations on external circumstances: too many people in too small a space, or too little money, or too busy a schedule. And perhaps these factors did exacerbate our conflicts. But we both knew there was a deeper problem, something far more fundamental. We feared that on our wedding day we had made the most devastating mistake of our lives.

L I clearly remember standing in our tiny living room at 2001 South Ashland, staring out the window at the evergreens, tears streaming down my cheeks.

'I can't believe I did this. How could I have been so stupid?'

I was angry, frustrated, fearful. It was like a terrible dream, but I couldn't wake myself up. I felt trapped and hopeless and confused. It suddenly seemed so obvious: I had married the wrong person.

What happened? I kept asking myself. *How did I get here? Where did I go wrong? And what do I do now?*

I shuddered under the shocking realization that the one I had pursued so earnestly, the man of my dreams, the person I had once feared I could never have, was now someone I wished I had never met. It was post-honeymoon blues at their worst. It was the ultimate buyer's remorse.

It was a terrible feeling, and sadly, one that is familiar to many. Almost every person who walks a wedding aisle comes to a point in the development of the marriage relationship when he or she says, 'I think I made a terrible mistake. I think I married the wrong person.'

Often people in the throes of fear and confusion say things like this: I don't feel like I know my spouse anymore. We had so much in common while we were dating, but now we seem to see everything differently. This isn't the person I fell in love with. My spouse has changed so much.

Actually, the spouse has probably changed very little. But reality often reveals what romance conceals. In the day-to-day routine of real life spouses begin to notice things they hadn't seen before. They tend to focus on their differences rather than the common beliefs or interests that drew them together, they tend to become irritated by the idiosyncrasies that charmed them when they were dating, and they tend to look at the negative side of the very qualities they most admired in one another before they were married.

That is what happened to us. During our courtship, our feelings flourished in the rich soil of our obvious compatibility. We held in common our deepest values and our highest goals. We respected one another. We enjoyed an intense whole-person attraction for one another. Our problem was that we focused all our attention on these delightful points

3

of contact and neglected to pay attention to some important points of difference. We didn't look at the differences in our family backgrounds, or the differences in our basic personalities.

Our failure to pay careful attention to our personality differences was a mistake for which we have paid a high price. We are convinced that the history of our marriage could have been written in far more pleasant terms if we had stumbled upon the ideas presented in this chapter during our courtship rather than fourteen years into our marriage.

Some of the ideas presented in the next few pages were previously discussed in *Honest to God?* (a book by Bill Hybels), in a chapter called 'Mutually Satisfying Marriage'. We think they are so important, however, that we decided to present them in an updated form in this chapter.

The Spice of Life

Experts in the field of personality development teach that just as human beings are born with blue eyes or brown eyes, with black hair or blond hair, tall or short, so they are born with predispositions towards certain ways of thinking, behaving, and viewing the world. In the 1950s Isabel Myers and Katharine Briggs expanded on Carl Jung's work on differing temperament traits and devised a test for identifying personality types based on varying combinations of these inborn traits. This test became known as the Myers-Briggs Type Indicator.

One book that takes an in-depth look at Jung's theory and the applications made by Myers and Briggs is *Please Understand Me* by David Keirsey and Marilyn Bates.[1] It has been of great help to us. By focusing on four aspects of thought and behaviour, this book has helped us see some of the different ways in which people approach thinking and behaving. These diverse ways of thinking or behaving are called preferences. Each preference spans a continuum from mild to moderate to extreme. If you find it easy to 'see yourself' in a given description on the following pages, you probably have an extreme preference in that area. If the picture isn't quite as clear, you may have only a mild preference.

The first potential difference deals with sources of emotional energy and how they affect people's relational patterns. Some people are *introverts* who derive energy from solitude. They enjoy spending lots of time alone and usually tend towards pursuits that afford quiet isolation. An extreme introvert might choose to go jogging alone rather than join an exercise class, and would be more likely to read a self-help book than attend a personal growth seminar. If you ever see anyone playing eighteen holes of golf alone, you can bet he or she is an introvert.

Introverts think before they speak and usually say little. They prefer a few close friends rather than many acquaintances, and would often opt for a quiet night at home rather than a social get-together. They may be warm, caring, and friendly towards people, but social interaction drains them – they feel slightly uncomfortable in groups – so they need a heavy balance of energizing solitude. They need to get alone where they can relax, 'let down', and be themselves again.

Extroverts, on the other hand, derive energy from interaction with people. Most extroverts enjoy working and playing in a team. They usually have many friends and spend much of their time with others. Extreme extroverts love nothing more than a party, and usually end up being the life of it. They tend to talk a lot; in fact, it sometimes seems they have to talk in order to figure out what they think. Extroverts enjoy solitude now and then, but too much of it drains them emotionally. They need the inspiration of interaction to keep their batteries charged.

One time after a flight, we were shuttled to our hotel by a middle-aged extrovert who generated a nonstop conversation for an hour and a half. When we asked him how he liked his job, he said, 'I love it. I spend twelve hours a day, six days a week, driving people back and forth from the airport. We have a great time, talking, joking, laughing, sharing stories. What could be better than that? I hate to go home at night.'

While introverts and extroverts differ in their approach to social interaction, sensers and intuitives differ in their approach to gathering and utilizing information. If *sensers* were to describe themselves in one word, it would probably be 'practical'. Sensing people 'want facts, trust facts, and remember facts'.[2] They have their feet firmly planted in reality. Giving little thought to what might have been or what may be in the future, they focus on what really happened or what is. They look to the past, learn through experience, and highly value other people's experiences. When 'sensing' employers interview potential employees, they tend to focus questions on the applicants' history, reasoning that past experience is the best basis for assuming future productivity.

Sensers are unusually accurate in observing detail because they prefer to take in information through their senses: what they see, hear, smell, feel, and touch. After parties sensers can often describe in accurate detail what all the guests wore, exactly how the room was decorated, and what songs played in the background. If asked to describe the event, extreme sensers would likely provide more details than many of their listeners would care to know.

Intuitives would probably describe themselves as 'innovative'. For them, what *is* can always be improved upon. Their vague sense of dissatisfaction with reality propels them towards change. The future intrigues them far more than the past or present, and they are fascinated with ideas and possibilities. Intuitive employers interviewing prospective employees tend to pay more attention to what the applicant says regarding the future of the organization than what he or she has done in the past.

Intuitives delight others with their speculation, imagination, creativity, and poetic imagery, but because their heads are often in the clouds, they are subject to error regarding facts and details. After parties, intuitives may well remember only those details related to their current preoccupation.[3] If asked to describe the evening, extreme intuitives would likely sum it up in a metaphor, and leave their sensing listeners feeling 'in the dark' and longing for more concrete information.

While sensers solve problems through careful analysis of the facts, intuitives often find complex solutions coming to them 'out of nowhere'. These frequent hunches lead intuitives down a variety of paths; in fact, they tend to skip from one activity to the next, often relying on others to finish what they started. They are often 'big-picture' people who need someone else – usually a senser – to fill in the details. Sensers often see intuitives as flighty, impractical, and unrealistic, while intuitives accuse sensers of being mired in minutiae and slow to see possibilities.

A third category – that of thinkers and feelers – shows how people differ in the area of assessing choices and making decisions. *Thinkers* take a logical approach to life, preferring to let their heads rule. They tend to be cool and calculated, cut and dried. They concern themselves with right and wrong, with prudence, with goals, with efficiency. In the legal system, they cry for justice. In business, for productivity and profit. In education, for unwavering truth. If something is right, they do it. If something is fair, they promote it. If something makes sense, they pursue it.

A manager who is a thinker says, with little trauma or emotion, 'I'm sorry, Joe. We've adjusted your job description three times, and you're still not making the grade. It will be better for the company and for you if you look for something else.' A teacher who is a thinker says, 'You should have stayed after school if you didn't understand the assignment.

I can't change your grade now. That would be unfair to the kids who did the assignment properly.' A parent who is a thinker says, 'Don't argue with me, Tony. You knew the rules and you broke them. Now you have to pay the consequences. I hope you learn your lesson.'

Feelers prefer to let their hearts rule. They feel deeply themselves and empathize easily with how others feel. They tend to base their decisions on how their choices will affect others. They hate it when people feel sad or hurt or discouraged, and long to be able to ease their pain. They prefer mercy over justice, put people ahead of profits, and sometimes see grey where thinkers see black and white.

Feelers in management agonize over difficult personnel decisions. 'Yes, you're right. Joe probably will be better off in another job. But he has tried so hard, and I hate to make him feel like a failure.' Feelers in education lose sleep over children who don't make the grade. 'I know Angela really doesn't deserve a better grade. But I hate to penalize her for misunderstanding the assignment.' Feelers who are parents really mean it when they say to their kids, 'This hurts me more than it hurts you.'

Thinking and feeling preferences have nothing to do with levels of intelligence or the ability to analyse and get to the root of complex issues. The question is: Once I see the issue, is it more natural for me to decide according to my head or according to my heart?

People also differ in how they structure their lives. Some people are highly organized and love lists and rules and schedules. They like to maintain a fairly predictable routine and can become irritated by interruptions. They like to know the plan and stick with the programme. Their motto is: *Just settle it.* They don't like surprises, and change can cause them anxiety. They tend to be serious and perfectionistic, and sometimes pessimistic. They are extremely conscientious, take responsibilities seriously, meet deadlines with time to spare, and seldom feel free to play until their work is done.

Other people feel trapped when life is organized, and prefer freedom and spontaneity. Their natural tendency is to play before they work, and some of them take their work seriously only when staring a deadline in the face. They hate to live by schedules and hesitate to finalize plans. Their motto is: *Play it by ear*. They like to keep as many options open for as long as possible. They thrive on change and unpredictability. They tend to be lighthearted, playful, and optimistic. They view every day as an adventure and can't wait to see what comes along.

B

My dad was the ultimate 'play it by ear' guy. One time when I had accompanied him to Washington, DC for business, he concluded his work with a few days to spare, so he suggested that we travel somewhere else.

'Where did you have in mind?' I asked.

'Well, Billy, what do you say we just walk into National Airport and get on the first plane to *anywhere*?'

That's exactly what we did! We missed the plane to London by about thirty seconds, but ended up in Jamaica, not a bad second choice.

The next two areas of difference, the initiator/responder[4] difference and the task/relationship difference, are not part of the Myers-Briggs Type Indicator, but we have found them to be helpful supplements. Bob Phillips explains them in his book *The Delicate Art of Dancing with Porcupines*.[5]

Initiators create ideas and action. They are aggressive, assertive, and willing to confront. They tend to be outspoken, often talking loudly and quickly, and adding emphasis with intonation and body language. Initiators make decisions easily, and express them with directness and intensity. They know how to take charge and like to do it. They can be excellent leaders, though they sometimes seem overwhelming to others.

Responders prefer to let other people's ideas and actions come their way. They are less assertive and aggressive than initiators, and avoid confrontations whenever possible. They are indecisive and cautious, and tend to speak quietly and unemotionally, hesitating to express their opinions for fear of imposing on others. They listen carefully, avoid the use of power if at all possible, and have a generally supportive attitude. Others view them as shy, but likeable.

The difference between initiators and responders is evident in a variety of situations. We have observed on our son's sports teams that children who are initiators tend to excel at offence, while responders often excel at defence. Young responders frequently seem to feel more comfortable defending their nets against oncoming soccer balls than trying to create action on the front line. Meanwhile, initiators seem to prefer the challenge of scoring goals.

People also differ in being either task oriented or relationship oriented. *Task-oriented* people tend to prioritize tasks above relationships. They feel best when they are accomplishing something tangible. If they are planning a dinner party, the details of the evening – food, decorations, seating arrangements, parking, entertainment – will be their primary concern. They will prefer to spend the evening attending to their organized list of nonrelational tasks.

Relationship-oriented people, on the other hand, place relationships ahead of tasks. When they plan a party, they hope someone else will handle the details, so they can greet the guests, make them feel at home, and spend the evening mingling.

Why Aren't You Normal Like Me?

This list is far from exhaustive. There is an almost infinite number of ways in which people can and do differ. And that is great. The intermingling of diverse personalities, unique outlooks, and complementary strengths is often the key to success in the marketplace, in education, in the church, in family life, and even in marriage.

The old adage about opposites attracting tends to be true, and for good reason. Opposites challenge one another, enhance one another, and, especially during courtship, fascinate one another. But the fascination often leads to frustration. Though we are drawn to people who are different from us, we have a hard time figuring them out. Eventually the mystery leads to misunderstanding, and too often the misunderstanding leads to maligning.

It can get downright ugly.

A previously adoring couple ends up trading blatant put-downs: *You don't make sense. You are strange. There is something wrong with you. Why aren't you normal like me?* The ultimate odd couple, they come to the only conclusion that seems to make sense: that they married the wrong person.

But did they? Would they really be better off if they had married someone just like them?

A Personal Case Study

B

I married Lynne because I respected her character and her spiritual commitment, I enjoyed the way we related as equals, and I was attracted to her physically. In addition, I was challenged and stimulated by our obvious differences. In nine out of ten areas of possible difference, we seemed to be at opposite ends of the continuum.

For example, Lynne was much quieter than I was and had fewer friends. She was warm and friendly towards people, but in groups she was reserved and preferred a few close friends rather than many casual acquaintances. She didn't talk a lot, but what she said was always worth listening to. I didn't know about introverts and extroverts back them. All I knew was that I was intrigued by the aura of substance, depth, and mystery that surrounded her.

She was also much more tender, caring, sensitive, and kind than I was. I knew I was off the charts as an unemotional, calculating thinker, and I thought I should probably have a heart someday. *Maybe it will help to marry one*, I thought. *Maybe we can just share hers*.

Lynne was also more structured and organized than me. For myself I preferred a more spontaneous approach to life, a make-it-up-as-you-go kind of approach, but I found her penchant for planning rather charming. Her life was very much in order; she was highly responsible; she knew how to cover the bases and handle the details and keep things running smoothly. It was fascinating to watch her in operation.

But several years into our marriage the fascination turned to frustration. I began to resent some of the very qualities that had attracted me to her initially.

To begin with, I decided she was *too* quiet. She was almost uncommunicative, it seemed to me. I had to draw everything out of her, and it was too much work. I wanted someone I could have easy conversations with. I wanted someone who didn't weigh every thought and word so carefully.

And she didn't have near enough friends. I kept trying to push her into relationships, but she wouldn't cooperate.

'I didn't know I was signing up to do duty with a hermit!' I shouted.

'Go away and leave me alone,' she whispered.

'That's the problem. You always want to be left alone. You always want *us* to be left alone. I want a social life. I want parties and picnics. I want Super Bowl bashes with so many people crammed together in the same room that they sweat!'

'You are sick! You superficial extroverts are all alike – a mile wide and an inch deep. You think the answer to everything is a party. Go ahead and invite the whole world over if you want to. Just don't invite *me*.'

She had a real problem in the relational/social area, but that wasn't her only one. She was also way too tender. Sensitivity and compassion are fine – in moderation. But she would sniffle through movies and sob if a friend's dog died.

And then there was the structure issue. She simply could not live with question marks. She always wanted to know the plan – like where we were going on vacation, when we were leaving, and when we were coming home – in advance!

That was just the beginning of my list of resentments. Our differences went on and on. I expressed some of my frustrations to Lynne in my world-renowned sensitive and constructive way. Others I kept inside where they could smoulder and create hostility. Both methods of dealing with them caused more harm than good, fuelled our already inflamed emotions, and broadened the distance between us.

But then God began chipping away at my self-centredness, my narrow-mindedness, and my immaturity. As He did that I began to see Lynne again through the eyes with which I had first seen her. And now I've come back full circle to a deep appreciation of the differences between us.

Because Lynne is an introvert our home is a safe and tranquil place. It is a refuge. My life is crowded to overflowing with people – neighbours, friends, colleagues, staff, church members – and involvements that stretch and drain me. If I came home to a flaming extrovert who wanted to throw a block party every three days I would go nuts.

Because Lynne enjoys time alone and loves to learn, she reads a lot. Then, what she reads she brings to our relationship. Not long ago on our Thursday morning breakfast date she told me about a book she was reading about what it was like to grow up in Europe during World War II. There I sat in that restaurant, getting a mini-course in history for the price of a bowl of oatmeal.

I see now that Lynne's ability to *feel* so deeply is what moves her to care for people in ways that are not natural for me. She is the one in our house who writes out the cheques to third-world ministries. She is the one who organizes blanket drives for people living in cardboard boxes. She is the one who dug ditches at an orphanage in Mexico. She is the one who pulls me aside after church services and tells me how my flippant remarks can pierce someone's soul. She is the one who has taught me how to treat our son, Todd, whose tender heart could have been crushed by my insensitivity.

I also need a wife who knows how to keep life in order. Thanks to Lynne's preference for structure, we have an organized home. We have clean clothes. We have a healthy diet. We have a budget that works. We have two children who know how to sit down and finish their homework. And I have to admit that some of our adventures have actually been enhanced by her thoughtful planning.

Many times I was tempted to take out a hammer and chisel and reshape Lynne into a replica of me. I even tried a little now and then. Thank God I didn't succeed. I realize now that one of me is plenty in our home. I bet one of you is plenty in your home too.

A Better Way

The hammer and chisel routine was a chore we shared. We each believed that we were the standard for what was right, normal, acceptable, even godly. And we each did our valiant best to get the other 'shaped up'. Then one year on holiday we read together that wonderful book on temperament we've previously cited called *Please Understand Me*. The title echoed our hearts' cries, and the content both chastised and encouraged us. We were chastised for our mutual arrogance in trying to force our preferences on each other. We were encouraged by the realization that we could both be right, normal, acceptable, and godly – even if we were opposite. We could be different without being wrong or right.

Reading that book marked a turning point in our relationship. We quit trying to minimize our differences, and decided to celebrate them instead. We decided to give each other the freedom to be who God made us to be.

L

Previously I had felt threatened by Bill's desire to spend so much time with other people. I thought that meant he wasn't happy with me. When I learned that extroverts need the stimulation of a variety of relationships, I could sincerely encourage him to enjoy his many friendships.

We also consciously focused on ways that our different perspectives and preferences complemented each other.

L

In the past I had judged Bill as cruel and heartless because he didn't empathize with others as easily as I did. I learned, however, that I could benefit from his more objective perspective. Sometimes I felt too sorry for people and 'rescued' them when I should have let them face the consequences of their mistakes. Bill helped me look beyond the immediate need to the future implications and the lessons people needed to learn. Conversely, Bill discovered that sometimes he needed to let my perspective soften him; he needed to let justice give way to mercy.

I have also learned from Bill to loosen up a little in regard to structure. I still generally prefer to plan ahead and maintain an orderly routine, but I've discovered that splashing the routine with a little spontaneity now and then can add fun to life and enhance relationships. This is particularly true in parenting. Some of the best times I have shared with my kids were spur-of-the-moment events I probably would have missed had

I not been influenced by Bill's make-it-up-as-you-go approach to life. Of course, there have been other wonderful parenting moments we both would have missed had I not carefully planned them.

Bill and I have found our initiator/responder differences to be especially complementary. Bill is the consummate initiator. He generates ideas and action without even trying, proposing far more options than he could ever develop on his own. I have energy and enthusiasm, but I often don't know where to channel them. We have discovered that we can be extremely productive as a couple when I throw my energy behind his ideas. This book is a prime example. So many times during the writing process, Bill tossed an idea into the air, and I caught it, developed it, and put it on paper. I could have thought for days and not come up with an idea as good as his. He could have played with his idea for days and never have developed it.

Discovering the complementary nature of previously frustrating differences is one of the surest indicators of a healthy marriage.

Not all differences are complementary, however. Sometimes instead of struggling to mesh our differences, we need to openly admit that they don't mesh and find creative ways to work around them. We discovered this in the realm of our Christian service.

L During the early years of our marriage we led couples' discipleship groups in our home. Bill loved it, but I always felt burdened by the responsibility of maintaining close, accountable relationships with five or six women each week. When we learned about the difference between introverts and extroverts we realized why I didn't enjoy, or feel effective, leading groups. After that, Bill began leading men's groups, and I focused on an area of service more in line with who God made me to be — writing articles on spiritual growth for the journal published by our women's ministry. The printed page proved to be a far more effective way for me to 'disciple' women than meeting in small groups.

Recently Bill mentioned this in a sermon. Afterward, a young couple approached him with tears in their eyes. 'I needed to hear this,' the husband said. 'I have been giving my wife a hard time for not joining me in an evangelistic marketplace ministry. She is always wanting to get involved with ministries to the poor, but I thought we should be serving together. Now I realize I was wrong. It's okay for me to do marketplace ministry, and her to serve the poor.'

A few weeks later I received a letter from the wife. She told me that her husband had just led several businessmen to the Lord, and that she had just joined a volunteer league that serves the inner-city homeless. 'We're both happy,' she said, 'and we each know that we are making a difference.'

It is still a challenge for us to give one another freedom to be ourselves. Sometimes we are nearly overwhelmed with the temptation to wield the chisel again. But then we remind ourselves that being opposite doesn't mean one of us is wrong. It just means we have to work a little harder to celebrate each other's uniqueness.

Your One and Only?

Why is it so important to understand that? Because sometimes when couples discover how different they really are, they jump to the conclusion that their marriage is hopeless, that they might as well give up because they chose the wrong spouse. Sometimes well-meaning Christians contribute to their sense of hopelessness.

We once heard a pastor say, 'Somewhere on planet earth there is a special someone just for you. God designed this person before the foundations of the world to be your lifetime mate.' This is the 'one and only' theory, and suggests that out of the five billion human beings that inhabit planet earth, God prepared one – and only one – to be your spouse.

This theory appears harmless, but it can be downright dangerous for a couple who are trying hard to make their marriage work, but making little headway. They are frustrated, but they keep plodding along until they stumble upon the 'one and only' theory. Suddenly a light bulb goes on. *Here's our problem. You're not my one and only, and I'm not yours. This marriage will never work. We missed. God can't bless this marriage, so why keep hitting our heads against brick walls? Let's part ways and find our one and only.* Their assumption is that if they find their one and onlys, marriage will be easy. They won't have to make compromises, or work through conflicts, or negotiate family differences, or wrestle with temperament issues. It will be smooth sailing on the seas of wedded bliss … if only they find their one and onlys. Even those whose convictions will not let them part ways live with the burden of regret. *I missed my one and only.*

While this notion has been bantered around in Christian circles for years, we find little biblical support for believing that God ordained every marital match before the foundation of the world. As in many other areas of Christian living, the Bible lays out broad parameters for spouse selection. Within those parameters, individuals have the freedom to choose. In 1 Corinthians 7:39 Paul says that a woman whose husband dies 'is free to marry anyone she wishes, but he must belong to the Lord'. Certainly Paul would tell her – and us – to choose carefully: to go through the proper checklists, move slowly, pray for guidance and sober judgment, and seek wise counsel. But then we are free to use our brains, examine our hearts, and select the spouse we feel best suits us. If we choose wisely, under His guidance, God promises the grace, courage, wisdom, and power needed to build our marriages.

If some years later we second-guess the wisdom of our choice, God says, 'Don't look backward. The decision has been made. Look forward. Face the challenges head on. I'll walk with you as you build this marriage. If it gets rough, seek help from friends. If you get stuck, see a counsellor. But don't waste time wondering if you missed your one and only. As far as I am concerned, *you are married to your one and only.* So get on with the task of making your marriage flourish. Turn to Me with humble hearts, and I'll help you. I'll give you wisdom and creativity. I'll teach you to compromise. I'll fill you with courage. I'll give you the strength to persevere.'

Building a flourishing marriage has been the most stretching challenge of our lives. It has pressed us into a relationship of dependence on God more than any other challenge we have faced. Our temperaments are so different. Our preferences are so contrary. Our styles are so incongruent. Our patterns are so diverse. Our outlooks are so varied. Our expectations are so conflicting. And while the challenge of meshing our differences has lessened over the years, it certainly hasn't disappeared. We spent the better part of last evening, in fact, struggling over a series of temperament-related hurdles, and went to bed exhausted from the effort.

But we each have so much that the other needs. We help to balance each other's extremes, to cover each other's weaknesses, and to complement each other's strengths. We enrich each other's lives with interests we would not otherwise pursue. We have forced each other to learn tolerance, and then appreciation, for a wide variety of people types; thus we have broadened each other's range of potential friendships, enhanced each other's ministry/career effectiveness, and enabled one another to effectively parent two very different children. Perhaps most importantly, we have prodded one another along the path towards Christlikeness.

Each time we have had to crane our necks to look through each other's eyes, or unclench our fists and resist the urge to fight, or prop our elbows on the table and lean forward and say, 'I was wrong', we have inched a tiny bit closer to the person we each want to become.

So we wake up each morning thankful for a marriage that challenges but enriches us, and reminds us every day that different isn't bad; it's only different.

Notes

1. Marilyn Bates and David Keirsey, *Please Understand Me* (Del Mar, CA: Prometheus Nemesis Book Company, 1984), p. 17.
2. Bates and Keirsey, *Please Understand Me*, p. 17.
3. Bates and Keirsey, *Please Understand Me*, p. 18.
4. *Initiators* and *responders* are our terms. Bob Phillips, author of *The Delicate Art of Dancing with Porcupines*, calls them tellers and askers.
5. Bob Phillips, *The Delicate Art of Dancing with Porcupines* (Ventura, CA: Regal Books, 1989).

Preparing for Conflict

'I don't believe it.'

'It's true. We have been dating for three years and we have never had a fight. What can I say? We were made for each other. What about you two? You've been dating for a long time. What's it been like for you?'

We were more than a little intimidated. How could we sit across the table from the perfect couple and spill the truth about our stormy romance and our broken engagement? Would it hurt to 'soften' the story a bit?

'Oh, we've had a few conflicts. But nothing major, and we've always been able to resolve them. Besides, we think it's healthy for dating couples to "go at it" now and then and learn to work things out. What better way to prepare for marriage?'

'Well, maybe that's true for you. But if we could make it through three years of dating without a problem, I don't see why we should expect trouble in marriage. We won't have the pressures of college, or living with our parents, or juggling part-time jobs. Marriage should be easy compared to what we're dealing with now. It'll be a snap.'

We wished them well and left the restaurant thinking that maybe they were right. Maybe marriage *would* be a snap for them. Maybe they could maintain their perfect record. They sure seemed like an ideal match.

But we – and they – were wrong. Establishing careers, maintaining a home, and just living with one another proved to be a bigger challenge than our friends had anticipated. They couldn't figure out how to divide household responsibilities. They discovered they had opposing perspectives on money. In-law tensions put them at odds. Colliding schedules caused frequent angry explosions. Sexual frustrations kept them awake at night. They couldn't agree on holiday plans…

And they desperately needed a holiday! They needed an escape from reality. After three years of marriage, they felt imprisoned by a solid wall of conflicts they did not know how to resolve. And inside the wall, the air was steaming with the heat of hostility.

Emergency

It is inexcusable that couples are allowed to marry without taking mandatory conflict resolution lessons. Yet it happens all the time. Teachers, pastors, parents, and friends sit idly by and watch starry-eyed lovers overdose on romance and infatuation, knowing full well that eventually reality will strike with a vengeance, conflicts will arise and hostilities brew, and the once blissful couple will face an emergency that neither partner will be prepared to face. Because they have not been coached or trained, they will have no emergency procedures to fall back on.

So what will they do? In most cases, they will resort to the only conflict resolution procedures they are familiar with: the ones their parents used. Even if they witnessed an unhealthy, unacceptable method of conflict resolution, and even if they vowed they would never behave that way, in the absence of proper training, they will almost inevitably revert to the method they grew up with.

Freeze 'Em Out

Some people fall back on the Eskimo style of handling conflict. In a home where this method is used, everyone knows there is a conflict; they can feel it in the air. But nobody talks about it. Everybody backs off, detaches, and mutters under their breath. No matter how large the problem looms, it is never dealt with openly. People negotiate around it, or avoid it, or hope that time will thaw things out. And sometimes the climate does warm up enough for people to start talking again. But the nice weather lasts only until the next conflict, which will probably focus on the same unresolved issue that caused conflict before. In family like this, nothing is ever really worked through.

In other Eskimo homes the chill never leaves the air. With each new conflict family members add another layer of ice. Eventually they freeze themselves into total withdrawal from one another.

Let the Bullets Fly

Some families handle conflict cowboy-style. When a problem surfaces or a misunderstanding arises, they square off and start shooting verbal bullets. 'This town ain't big enough for the two of us,' they announce. Then they shout and throw things and break windows in the saloon. Intimidation is the name of the game. Feelings are ventilated. Anger is released. There is action and drama. But a lot of damage is done along the way. Feelings are hurt and children hear things they should never have to hear.

And the issues that drove people apart remain unresolved.

Let Me Out of Here

Some people deal with conflict by escaping. A family conflict arises, so someone goes out and gets drunk. Another escapist might go on a shopping spree. Somebody else takes drugs. Or walks out for two or three days. Another out is workaholism. The trauma of the self-destructive escapes or the thoughtless disappearing acts tends to cloud the original issue. There is relief when the husband quits drinking or when the wife finally comes home. The problem hasn't been solved, but at least the escapist is home and under control. Until the next conflict.

In escapist families there is plenty of action: doors slamming and people coming and going. But it is conflict avoidance at its best. Issues are never faced, and problems are never solved.

I Don't Know What Happened

Sadly, some people react to conflict by manhandling others. They allow verbal assault to escalate into physical violence, and they create more pain and distance than the original issue could possibly have caused.

Young people who grew up in violent homes usually vow to break that pattern of pain. But too often violence breeds violence. In spite of their good intentions, they resort to what they know. When calamities befall, or frustrations rise, or anger boils, or conflicts rage, or emotions scream for release, they respond reflexively. They lash out; they lose control; they strike.

Later they say, 'I don't know what happened. Why did I do that?' The answer is no mystery. In the absence of proper conflict management training, they did the only thing they knew to do. They did what came naturally. The cycle of violence can be broken, but it usually won't be without proper training.

Mandatory Training

Too often relationships that begin with promise end with pain. In the daily rounds of reality, disagreements surface and personalities clash. Harsh words lead to broken trust and hurt feelings. Hidden hostilities choke romance. And a cloud of relational sorrow hangs menacingly overhead. If the pattern continues, the marriage dissolves and another plot is purchased in the relational cemetery.

If we could make this chapter mandatory reading we would. Even the most wisely matched couples will face conflicts in marriage. How they handle them will determine whether their relationship survives or ends up marked with a granite tombstone.

Prerequisite for Survival

Most people whose marriages have failed have a ready answer when asked about the demise of their relationship. They blame it on adultery or alcoholism or abuse. They accuse their spouses of dishonesty or insensitivity or irresponsibility. They claim irreconcilable differences or personality conflicts. But such answers don't fit the question. While these factors may cause hurts and disappointments and complications, they are not enough to kill a marriage.

You see, we have witnessed many marriages that have survived the above-mentioned problems. Many have not only survived, but have gone on to flourish. On the other hand, we have known couples who encountered mere tremors of difficulty, but their marriages ended up in the relational graveyard.

What makes the difference? Why are some relationships resistant and resilient and others so susceptible to infection and terminal diseases?

We have observed that in addition to knowing practical tools for conflict resolution, nearly all couples who survive the minor and major conflicts of married life have discovered a key antidote for marital demise. It is called *the spirit of reconciliation*. This elixir produces a heart condition that predisposes people towards reconciliation and revolutionizes the way they approach conflict.

For many people the normal reaction to relational hurt, misunderstanding, or attack is to strike back. To get even. To fix blame. To say, 'It's your fault.'

We have all behaved that way on occasion. What's more, we have probably felt justified. *What's right is right*, we say. *If you get hurt you gotta get even. I shouldn't have to put up with this. Retaliation is self-preservation.* Then we self-righteously spin on our heels and walk out the slammed door, straight to the relational graveyard. We can't stand the discomfort and turmoil of relational tension, and we see no way to fix it. So we get out the shovel, bury the relationship, and try to get on with life. But we live with a dull, aching pain that won't go away.

Scripture tells us that we were created to live in harmony and community with others. We were created for peace. That is why walking through our relational graveyards causes us so much grief. And why we need to trade in our spirit of retaliation for the spirit of reconciliation.

How do we do that? First, we need to acknowledge that we have fallen short of the moral standards of our holy God and that we are therefore in conflict with Him. Some of us do a pretty good job of not thinking about this, but most of us, during our semi-annual moments of introspection, get a little nervous about someday standing before a holy God. We feel a bit uneasy. We sense a latent fear of reprisal or punishment. And we know we can't do anything to escape it. Our past sins won't disappear, and God's holiness won't change. So we are stuck in an unresolvable and unwinnable conflict.

Coming to grips with our desperate position is the first step towards a spirit of reconciliation. The second step is to realize that God, 'being rich in mercy', offered His Son, Jesus Christ, to bridge the chasm of conflict that separates us from God. Through Jesus' death and resurrection, we can be reconciled to God and freed from the fear of condemnation and eternal death. We can be adopted into God's family and relate to Him as a much-loved child relates to a kind father.

The third step towards a reconciling spirit happens naturally to those who have been adopted into God's family and are growing spiritually. The joy of divine reconciliation begins to spill over into other areas of their lives. They want to experience the peace and harmony they enjoy with God with others. They begin to understand that all people – friends, family members, strangers, even enemies – matter to God. The chunks of ice in their chests begin to melt, and they feel concern and compassion for people they previously ignored or spurned or mistreated.

A Radical Remake

The Bible tells of a wealthy tax collector who routinely ripped people off without the slightest appearance of remorse – until he had a heart-to-heart with Jesus Christ over an unscheduled dinner. After a simple meal and a brief conversation, this hard-hearted extortionist emerged from his house a transformed man. With trembling lips he begged the forgiveness of those he had cheated, and promised to repay them four times over. He even vowed to give half of all his future earnings to the poor.

Obviously something supernatural happened at that dinner table. Not only was a sinner reconciled to God, but he also received the spirit of reconciliation, which turned his feelings towards people upside down. And what happened to Zacchaeus is the norm for all who become reconciled to God. The Holy Spirit plants within them an appreciation for others that wasn't there before. He gives them a longer fuse, more patience, an increased capacity to forgive, a heightened desire for harmony, a sensitivity and tenderness that they never felt before.

B

I know this is true. Before I became reconciled with God, I rarely lost sleep over relational conflicts. If I was involved in a private war with somebody, I enjoyed the challenge of making sure I won. If a person claimed to have a problem with me, I assured them that it was their problem. If someone said they didn't like me, I boasted that I didn't care. If I learned I had hurt someone's feelings, I assumed they were overly sensitive. If a relationship seemed destined to die – well, I didn't mind a funeral now and then.

I had a hard heart towards relational problems. I had a spirit of retaliation, of rebellion. I was usually convinced that I was right, and if any doubts surfaced I was quick to submerge them. I was not about to eat crow, or go crawling back on my hands and knees to seek reconciliation.

But then I was broken by an awareness of my sin, and humbled by God's willingness to adopt me into His family. The Holy Spirit began to chip away at my hard heart. 'Be tender,' he said. 'Swallow your pride. Rearrange your values. Be done with hostility. Seek peace. Reconcile.'

When the spirit of rebellion reigns in a marriage, every little conflict escalates into a war of harsh accusations. But when the spirit of reconciliation prevails even major conflicts can be discussed constructively and worked through.

After hearing a sermon on reconciliation, a young Marine broke down in tears and said, 'Somebody has to lead me to Christ right now. My marriage is in trouble, and I'm sick and tired of trying to fix it on my own. I can't do it. My wife can't do it. We try, but then we get defensive and rebellious. We need to be transformed. We need the spirit of reconciliation. Please help us.'

That young couple's marriages was like so many today: destined for the relational graveyard because the wrong spirit prevailed. Some of you may be a bit impatient reading this section. *This is supposed to be a book on marriage*, you say, *not a book on spiritual growth*. But spiritual growth is key to marriage because it is key to the spirit of reconciliation. During our courtship and the early years of our marriage, we were not aware of the practical steps for conflict resolution that we are going to suggest in the next chapter. Had we known them we could have avoided much pain and tension. But at least we both had the spirit of reconciliation. And that kept us working even when the work go so hard, and talking even when the talk seemed to accomplish so little. In spite of our relational difficulties, we refused to rush to the graveyard. Our heart condition drove us towards reconciliation.

It is not enough for one spouse to have a spirit of reconciliation. Both spouses must approach peace negotiations with a willingness to lay down their weapons, admit their mistakes, and work through to a solution. Then they can move successfully through the practical steps to conflict resolution.

Before turning to the next chapter, it may be helpful for you to discuss with your spouse the conflict resolution styles used in the families you grew up in. We also suggest that the two of you talk openly about the spirit of reconciliation. If you don't have it, please reread this chapter and consider become reconciled with God. Establishing peace with Him is the most important step you can take, both for you as an individual, and for your marriage.

Planning Peace Talks

In the previous chapter we mentioned that during the early years of our relationship we were not very good at resolving conflicts. That was a gross understatement. We had the spirit of reconciliation, but absolutely no clue about how to translate that spirit into practical action.

L

I took the Eskimo approach to handling conflict, which fit my introverted temperament perfectly. If Bill did something that hurt or angered me, I registered the offence on my mental tally card and proceeded to freeze him out. I still talked to him, of course, but only when necessary. And I never looked him in the eye, or smiled, or said anything truly pleasant. I pouted. I sighed. I walked around the house looking like my dog had just died.

When Bill asked me what was wrong, I would look at the floor and say, 'Nothing.'

'Oh, come on,' he'd beg. 'I know something is wrong. Tell me.'

If he pressed hard enough, I would finally reveal my hidden hurt. If he gave up too soon, I'd tuck it deeper inside.

My unwillingness to communicate honestly was very frustrating to Bill. He though I was being childish, or trying to punish him for offending me. Sometimes he was right, but more often than not I was just confused. I couldn't understand why his behaviour bothered me, so I hesitated to mention it. Or I didn't think I was justified in being upset, so I tried to pretend I wasn't. Sometimes I just didn't know how to shape my feelings into words. But regardless of the reason, my failure to communicate openly and clearly often chilled the atmosphere in our home.

Bill didn't do much better than I did, though he took the opposite approach. He is by nature a confronter and has little trouble verbalizing his thoughts, so he became a controlled cowboy. He didn't shout or throw things, but he was a sharpshooter with his words. While I insisted on burying anger, he insisted on letting it fly.

For us, facing conflict became a cultural experience. The cowboy fired his pistol and the Eskimo turned to ice. It was like a Broadway production. But neither of us applauded, and both of us got hurt.

It is bad enough that faulty methods of conflict resolution seldom resolve the conflict. What is worse is that they often heap hurt upon hurt. A couple expends an enormous amount of energy trying to work through a problem, and they end up in a worse state than when they started. Is it any wonder many couples give up trying to settle their differences?

Many times, in the aftermath of soured conflict negotiations, we felt like giving up. But time after time the spirit of reconciliation prevailed, and instead of giving up we read another book, or listened to another tape, or talked to another friend. And eventually we came up with a plan for resolving conflicts that really works.

Is That a Plank in Your Eye?

The first step in our conflict resolution plan is to pray about the problem. It is amazing how many insurmountable conflicts get whittled down to a manageable size in the woodshed of prayer.

While our human tendency is to cast blame on others and deny personal guilt, the Holy Spirit has an amazing way of bringing a more balanced perspective. In the Sermon on the Mount Jesus challenged His followers to point their fingers at themselves before pointing them at others. 'Why,' He asked, 'do you look at the speck of sawdust in your brother's eye and pay no attention to the plank in your own eye? How can you say to your brother, "Let me take the speck out of your eye," when all the time there is a plank in your own eye? You hypocrite, first take the plank out of your own eye, and then you will see clearly to remove the speck from your brother's eye' (Matthew 7:3–5).

What does this say to spouses? It tells us that every time we feel slighted, offended, taken advantage of, or hurt, before we take out the guns and start shooting, or run away, or freeze someone out, we need to get alone with God and ask some probing questions. *Am I the problem here? Am I being unreasonable or selfish or insensitive? Am I aggravating the situation? Am I yielding to sin?*

We can each recall numerous times when we thought the other was totally out of line. We were each convinced that the evidence was on our side. One wore the white hat and the other the black. But so often in prayer our eyes were opened to an entirely different picture. We became aware of false assumptions we had been making. Of judgmental attitudes we had been harbouring. Of impatience. Of insensitivity. Of intolerance. So many times we have been on the verge of 'straightening each other out', only to find that we were the ones who needed to be straightened out. With God's help, each of us has resolved many so-called marital conflicts without ever having to involve our spouse.

We believe that the tension in most marriages could be cut in half if spouses would pray every day about their marriages. God does miracles when people pray. Lives are changed and hearts softened when people pray. Pointing fingers change direction when people pray. Problems shrink when people pray. Sometimes, conflicts even disappear when people pray.

L | Many years ago, Bill and I decided to set aside Thursday night as our date night. However, more often than not, Bill ended up with a scheduling conflict, and I ended up spending our date night alone. I was tempted to accuse Bill of being careless, but as I prayed about the problem, I realized we had simply chosen a bad time. For a pastor, evening hours are the hardest hours to protect. I suggested that we move our date 'night' to Thursday morning and see what happened. It worked. Because we are both morning people, we have actually enjoyed Thursday mornings more than we ever enjoyed Thursday nights. God's idea was much better than ours.

So, before you go to your spouse, go to God. See what wisdom and insight He has to offer.

Can We Talk?

The next step is to plan a formal peace conference in a quiet, unrushed setting where you and your spouse can face the issue head on.

'Come on,' you say, 'don't sell us short. We talk about our marriage problems. I pass through the family room and give a few shots. My spouse nags and complains at the dinner table. We may get a little sarcastic, a little small now and then. But we know what the issues are. We know how to go after each other.'

Maybe you do know what the issues are. But there is a big difference between 'going after each other' and really solving problems. We have found that serious conflict can seldom be worked out in the cracks of life. You can't do it on the run, or when the kids are climbing all over you, or as you are drifting off to sleep at night. You need to plan a peace conference in a neutral setting when you both have optimal energy.

It is also important to schedule peace talks as soon as possible. Paul says, 'Do not let the sun go down while you are still angry' (Ephesians 4:26). His words suggest daily peace talks for conflicts that have arisen in the course of that day. Busy schedules sometimes make that impossible, and serious issues may require more formally scheduled peace talks, but even those should be scheduled as soon as possible. In the meantime, couples must covenant together not to 'sin in their anger'. They must both refrain from the kind of 'cheap shots' – sarcasm, innuendo, and rudeness – that inevitably complicate the issues. We call this delicate period of time between recognizing a problem and resolving it 'the commitment phase', and we will discuss it more in a later chapter.

Often, a portion of our Thursday morning date is devoted to a peace talk. We go to a local restaurant, sit in a booth in a dark, secluded corner, and spread the issues out on the table. Resolving conflicts has a remarkable way of draining relational tension and drawing people together, so by the time we finish the peace talk we are usually in a great mood to enjoy the rest of the morning.

People who are night people should plan their peace talks over a quiet dinner. Others would do well to schedule lunch appointments. If you have small children, we suggest hiring a baby-sitter or trading baby-sitting services with a friend, so your peace talks can be unrushed and undisturbed.

But let's say you have scheduled the peace talk and you are seated across the table from one another. Now what?

Begin with Affirmation

We used to jump right into the problem, which meant we were starting the discussion from a negative position. Doing that almost always polarized us and elicited defensive responses.

Learning to begin with affirmation helped us start our discussions from a positive position. Doing that softened the blow of the conflict and kept us from reeling into defensiveness. Our peace talks became much more peaceful when we learned to say, 'Honey, I love you and I am committed to our marriage. But I think it can be better than it is. Here are some ideas I have.'

An introduction like that can lead to a constructive conversation.

Be Willing to Take Blame

Bring to the meeting the insights and attitudes that were fostered during your time of private prayer. Acknowledge specifically how you contributed to the tension. Do not take blame you don't deserve, but fully accept what is rightly yours.

'I should never have said what I said.'
'I'm sorry I was so selfish.'
'Forgive me for letting my ego get in the way.'
'I feel horrible about blowing up in front of the kids.'
'I've been expecting too much from you.'
'It was unfair for me to think you could read my mind.'
'I didn't communicate clearly. I'm sorry I misled you.'

You will be amazed at the power of apology. Two short words – I'm sorry – have saved business partnerships, reconciled neighbours, reunited fathers and sons, and rescued marriages that were headed for the graveyard. There is no magic in the words themselves, but when they are said sincerely they reveal what is underneath – the spirit of reconciliation. And they open up the lines of communication.

When Zacchaeus, the reformed tax collector, ran out into the streets, the people who knew him probably ran in the opposite direction. 'How is he going to cheat us this time?' they wondered. 'What new scam has he concocted?' But apparently he stopped them dead in their tracks. How? He said, 'I'm sorry. I was wrong. I cheated you. I want to make it right.' They were probably suspicious; they probably had a wait-and-see attitude. But like most people, they wanted to believe the best. So they listened. They opened their hearts. And Zacchaeus' apology opened the way for healing and restitution.

Express Hurt Instead of Hostility

Most problems start with hurt. A wife feels hurt because her husband didn't ask about a presentation she made at work that day. Or because he forgot their anniversary. Or was unnecessarily critical of her mother. A husband feels hurt because his wife didn't notice the weight he lost. Or because she wasn't sensitive about a pressure at work. Or she insulted him in front of a friend.

Hurt is a legitimate response to disappointment and offence, and it should never be denied or kept hidden inside. It should always be expressed and discussed. But hurt becomes a problem when people let it build up inside and turn into anger. The wife starts out being hurt by her husband's apparent lack of interest in her career, but after she mulls the hurt around in her mind for a while it becomes infected. She ends up being angry at 'the insensitive louse who only cares about what he does'.

This is why it is important to plan peace talks as soon as possible, before hurt turns to anger. Most people are moved by another person's pain, so revealing hurt can build bridges of understanding and compassion. But ventilating hostility blows up bridges, because people are repelled by angry assaults. When someone attacks, our natural reaction is to fight back.

Another mistake that causes hurt to turn to anger is accumulating grievances. One hurt is manageable. You can keep it under control, express it constructively, and work through it. Two hurts are a little harder to deal with. Accumulate more than that and it is almost impossible to keep them from comparing notes and deciding that they deserve to turn into anger.

During the early years of our marriage we repeatedly accumulated piles of grievances. Eventually we became so full of anger we exploded and said all kinds of destructive things. Even Eskimos can reach the boiling point if the hidden hurts simmer long enough.

So please deal with grievances as they arise. Don't stack them on top of one another or let them fester inside until they turn to hostility. Anger is always a secondary emotion. If spouses back up to what preceded it, they will often find hurt. If they reveal the hurt, they will weaken the walls that separate them.

Make Direct Statements

Hints and offhand remarks accomplish little. Whether we are in the midst of a formal peace talk or a casual conversation, we must say what we mean.

L I don't know why, but I had a hard time with this one. It was much easier for me to say, 'It sure has been a long, busy day. What a drag to have to cook dinner tonight,' than to say, 'Bill, I have had a rough day and I don't have the energy to cook dinner. I would really like to go out tonight.' Of course, if Bill didn't pick up on my hint and suggest that we go out for dinner, I thought he was insensitive and unconcerned about my needs.

I had to work hard on stating my desires and frustrations honestly and clearly. During peace talks, that means saying, 'I was upset because you didn't call to tell me you would be late,' rather than saying, 'I think husbands should be more respectful of their wives' schedules.' I need to own my thoughts and feelings and express them in specific terms. It is much easier for us to deal with something honest and concrete like my disappointment about Bill not calling me, than to deal with a vague generality about husbands and wives and respect.

Make 'I Feel' Statements

Many peace plans are sabotaged by *you* statements of accusation that antagonize spouses and often terminate the peace process before it even starts.

'You don't help enough around the house.'
'You spend too much time at work.'
'You don't know how to handle money.'
'You are insensitive.'

I feel statements are much less inflammatory and open the door for further discussion and practical problem solving.

'I feel overwhelmed by household responsibilities. I have thought of some ways we might be able to divide up the tasks. Can I tell you about them?'

'I often feel left out of your life because you spend so much time at work. Can we talk about that?'

'I feel frustrated about our financial situation. Would you be willing to discuss some ways to keep our budget in better order?'

'I felt hurt by your comments this morning. You probably didn't mean to offend me, but let me tell you how I felt.'

Avoid 'Never' and 'Always'

L I am an extremist. To me there is no middle ground. Life is black or white, happy or sad, up or down, wonderful or terrible. Unfortunately, this perspective tends to colour my communication patterns. Too often I speak in exaggerated terms.

'You never come home on time.'
'You always forget to call.'

'You are forever leaving dirty dishes in the family room.'

I may have a perfectly reasonable concern, but if I express it in extreme terms, I invalidate it. I turn the truth into a lie. Does Bill *never* come home on time? Does he *always* forget to call? Is he *forever* leaving dirty dishes in the family room? Well ... about the dishes.

If we want our grievances to be taken seriously we must make accurate, truthful, realistic statements. *Always* and *never* will always – well, almost always – shift the focus away from the real issue. The unreasonably accused spouse will probably dismiss the original concern and blame the relational tension on the other spouse's poor communication techniques.

I Have an Idea!

So, come to the peace talks with a spirit of reconciliation. Affirm your relationship and be quick to say, 'I'm sorry.' Express hurts instead of hostilities. And make direct, realistic 'I feel' statements.

Then commit yourself to being solution centred. A husband once told us, 'Well, I did what you suggested. I took my wife out for a peace talk. But it didn't help. I told her what I thought; she told me what she thought. Then we went home with our basket load of accusations. What good did that do?' It did no good because they weren't solution centred. They each presented their case and hoped the other would give in. A better approach would have been to sit down at the table and ask, 'How can we compromise? How can we adjust and adapt? What would be a mutually satisfactory alternative?'

If spouses have spent time in prayer prior to the meeting, they probably already have possible options in mind, or even listed on paper. They can bring these ideas to the peace talk, not as definite answers to the problem, but as starting points, as possibilities to be reshaped and refined together.

We used to argue over money. 'Why did you spend money on *that*?' 'But I thought we were saving for *this*.' 'You said we had to be frugal this month, and now look what you bought.' Finally we decided we needed to agree on a yearly budget. So we prayed for flexibility and open-mindedness, then sat down and hammered out a budget that we signed and vowed to stick with. Every January we update and revise it, and we haven't had a serious budgeting conflict in years.

We had similar conversations regarding scheduling. Because our schedules were so unbalanced during the early years of our marriage, we both experienced major hurt and frustration in this area. Eventually we had to work out a plan detailing how many nights we could be gone each week, how much travelling we could do, when we should schedule our weekly date, and what to do when scheduling commitments overlap. Establishing mutually agreed upon guidelines freed us from constant disagreements and disappointments.

Moment of Truth

We have discovered that problems which caused either of us a high degree of hurt in the past, or problems that require complex solutions, have the potential to bring out the worst in us, even during peace talks. In such cases, we have to work very hard not to undermine the peace process.

B   During one particularly difficult discussion, Lynne and I were following the steps for conflict resolution as best we could, but a resolution was not coming easily. No leaflet had dropped from heaven with a three-point plan printed on it. No ideas

were popping full-blown into our minds. We were both beginning to realize that we felt more strongly than we had thought
about the items on our individual agendas. We were trying to
compromise, but we were both being stretched – farther than
we had anticipated.

Eventually, pride started to surface, evil forces began to
rear their ugly heads, and the dark side of my humanity decided to play its card. Flashing across the screen of my imagination was a scene from a television movie I had just seen.
A husband and wife were faced off in a heated verbal assault.
The lights cast a sinister glow, the camera zoomed in, the
music built to a crescendo, and at the height of emotional
intensity, the husband blasted his wife with deadly words,
turned on his heels, and left the room – slamming the door
behind him. That image flashed on my mental screen and
I thought, *that's what I want to do! It would feel so good to let
loose a verbal barrage and slam a door.*

But I knew that while that kind of behaviour makes for
good Nielsen ratings, it makes for bad marriages. On top of
that, it's a cowardly response to conflict. It takes far more
courage to fight pride and evil desires than it takes to fight my
wife. When you're in the thick of battle, it's so easy to be a
jerk. It's so easy to let your frustrations fly, to give free rein to
your anger, to be petty and immature. But those times are
moments of truth. Inside you want to be childish, you want
the easy way out, you want to win. But the Holy Spirit is
cheering for you to do what's right. 'Control yourself. Stick
with the process. Don't deny your feelings, but express them
constructively. Negotiate. Compromise. Reconcile.' Who you
listen to in those moments of decision reveals your character
and courage.

I've heard men say, 'I had a fight with the old lady. Boy, did
I tell her …' And I think, *Do you really believe it takes valour to
leave a peace talk, slam a door, and then brag about it to your
friends? Do you really think I'm impressed?*

What takes courage is to stay at the table and say, 'We made an inch of progress today. Maybe tomorrow we can move forward another inch. But we won't give up until we solve this problem.'

Would You Help Us, Please?

But what if your peace talks aren't working? What if you can't stay on track? What if you constantly go forward one inch and back two? The next step is to seek counsel from a trusted friend or couple. Proverbs 11:14 says, 'For lack of guidance a nation falls, but many advisers make victory sure.' We shudder to think where we would be without the wise, insightful, and sometimes painful counsel we have received from trusted friends.

We are not talking her about golf buddies or bridge partners. Nor do we advocate gossip sessions where one spouse complains about the other. We are talking about trusted and respected friends, and about constructive conversations in which we seek counsel not about our spouse's behaviour, but about our own.

B

A close friend once told me, 'You're too frugal with your wife. You're liberal when it comes to giving to God's work. You're liberal with your kids. You're liberal when your friends are in need. But you're pretty cheap with your wife. You need to be more generous with her.'

Another friend said, 'You're more demanding with your wife than you think you are. You expect too much from her. You need to give her a little slack.'

One said, 'You ought to take more interest in your house and yard. You enjoy having an orderly, well-maintained refuge to come home to, but you don't take enough responsibility for keeping it that way.'

I didn't like hearing those things, but I needed to hear them. They were true, and they were building walls in my relationship with Lynne. I'm thankful I had friends who knew me and loved me enough to take the risk of telling me the truth. And I'm thankful that I had learned the value of accepting hard counsel.

We have also benefited from seeking counsel together from another couple. 'What advice can you give us about this situation?' we ask. 'How do you compromise in this area? How have you solved this problem?' At times we have had to schedule formal peace talks with our friends. Sometimes we just use casual get-togethers as opportunities to glean insight from married couples we respect.

Call in the Professionals

But what if you haven't established accountable relationships with friends? What if there are no couples with whom you both feel comfortable sharing? Or what if they have tried to help you, but they can't? Then please go to a counsellor.

For the most part, contemporary Americans are counsel-crazy. We think nothing of hiring a consultant to help with management problems, or an accountant to help with finances. We don't hesitate to take our medical problems to doctors or our legal questions to lawyers. We willingly go to nutritionists for dietary advice, and to colour analysts to find out how we should dress. But if someone suggests going to a marriage counsellor we say, 'In a heaven, I'll go! I can handle my household. I don't need help. Not me. No way.'

Some people refuse to seek counsel because they are embarrassed; they don't want anyone to know their marriage is a bit frayed around the edges. Some people refuse because they are afraid to face a painful truth, or afraid of what they might learn about themselves or their spouse. Others refuse because they are stubborn and cruel. They would rather dismantle the emotional health of their spouse than expend the energy to get help. Still others question the theological 'rightness' of seeking professional counsel. 'Shouldn't we be able to pray ourselves out of this problem? Shouldn't we be able to find an answer in the Bible?'

We believe that prayer and Bible study are important elements in marital health. We also believe, however, that God has gifted certain individuals with a degree of discernment, knowledge, and wisdom that allows them to assist couples who occasionally hit impasses, or couples who are stuck in unhealthy, destructive patterns of relating.

Some couples get stuck for so long they forget what a good marriage is like. They begin to settle for a mediocre marriage, or even for a miserable one. They need somebody to refresh their minds and teach them how to get back to a healthy, positive, loving way of relating.

Sometimes only one spouse is willing to seek counsel. We encourage that partner to go alone. It is better for one partner to get unstuck than for both to remain where they are. We have seen God do amazing things through one spouse who is willing to face the challenge of growth. Many times the unwilling spouse is impacted by the visible change in the other.

Conflict resolution requires courage and persistence. It calls for humility and honesty. It chips away at our hardness of heart, and sometimes it produces pain. But it is always worth whatever effort it takes, whatever inconvenience it causes, and whatever change or compromise it requires.

Whatever Happened to Romance?

L Several years into our marriage a casual conversation with a male acquaintance awakened me to a serious problem in our marriage. Over lunch in a local restaurant Bill and I listened while this middle-aged consultant for an international manufacturing firm lamented having to spend so much time away from his wife.

'I make the best of it though,' he said. 'I call her every night and we talk about what happened during the day. I send her lots of little notes and cards, just to remind her I'm thinking about her. If I travel to interesting places I buy her jewellery that is representative of the area. And I always come home with lingerie – something fun and flirtatious that puts us in the mood for romance. We have to be apart so often, we want to make the time we have together count!'

He mentioned his wife several other times during the conversation, and it became obvious that after twenty-five years of marriage he was still 'crazy in love' with her. He still treasured her. He still looked forward to being with her. He still had fun with her. He still got a kick out of making love to her.

As I listened, I found myself being strangely attracted to this man, and it frightened me. I didn't understand it. There I was, sitting next to my handsome, successful young husband to whom I was wholeheartedly committed. Yet I was feeling drawn to a fiftyish grandfather who talked nonstop about his wife. What was going on?

Throughout the afternoon I pondered the conversation and finally realized that the reason I felt drawn to that man was that I longed to be loved and treasured the way he loved and treasured his wife. I wanted to feel special, to be pursued, to know that my husband delighted in me – and that wasn't happening in our marriage at that point.

It is happening in our marriage now, and you will see how the change came about in the next chapter. But before the romantic rebirth of our marriage, Bill and I had many difficult conversations. The evening of our talk with the businessman, I described for Bill what I had felt during lunch and what I had learned during the afternoon.

'I love you, Bill, and I am more committed to our marriage than I have ever been. But we've lost something along the way. Our marriage seems more like a business, a partnership, a joint venture, than like an intimate, loving union. We struggle along, trying to live in peace as best we can, but there is too little spark in our relationship. Too little fun. Too little romance. I don't want to go on like this any more. Marriage should be so much more than this. We should be so much happier than we are. We need to get the romance back.'

We need to get the romance back. We have heard so many spouses make that statement. Couples who are unhappy with their marriages often admit that what disturbs them more than anything is the lack of romance. *If I married the right person,* a spouse asks, *why did the courtship end so abruptly after the wedding? Why did the flames die so quickly? Why is there so much less 'feeling' in our marriage than there used to be?*

Few couples expect to maintain the intense, super-charged, adolescent-style relationship that marked the height of their courtship. In fact, most couples feel somewhat relieved when life begins to settle into a more normal routine, and they can get about the tasks of real life again. But many marriages settle down too much. Within a few short years the sparkle has faded completely. Feelings have become mere memories. Romance has become something to read about in cheap novels. Spouses relate like roommates who share an occasional one-night stand. And together they face thirty more years of disappointment and frustration.

What Pulls the Plug on Romance?

A number of factors drain the romance out of marriage. One is the curse of familiarity. It happens in all arenas of life. You buy a new car and for a few weeks you create reasons to go to the store so you can drive it. You wash it on lunch break. You make your kids shower before they get near it. But after a while, without even realizing it, you begin treating your new car the way you treated the old one. You let the dog crawl around in it. You let the kids drink milk shakes in it. You say, 'I don't have to worship this. It's just a car.'

The same thing happens when you buy a new house, a new piece of furniture, or a new item of clothing. For a while you treat it so carefully, but once the shine wears off and the glitter fades — once familiarity sets in — you quit protecting it and worrying about it and caring for it so meticulously.

Unfortunately, we often treat people the same way we treat purchases. During the courtship phase, when a guy arrives to pick up his girlfriend for a date, he barely touches the doorbell before the door swings wide open and she says, 'Oh Tom, I've been thinking about you all day. I've been counting the ticks of the clock. I thought you would never arrive.' After two years of marriage, Tom comes home from work forty-five minutes late and announces, 'I'm home, honey.' His wife says, 'So am I. What do you want, a marching band?'

A twisted sense of security can also drain the romance out of marriage. During the courtship phase, partners live with the nagging fear that if they don't stay on their toes, if they aren't thoughtful and courteous, if they don't communicate creatively, if they don't 'beat the competition', they might lose the relationship. Once they are married, however, some people get a little too complacent. They feel a little two secure. They get careless, thoughtless, and matter-of-fact about their relationship.

Physical exhaustion can also drain the romance out of marriage. When do most people have their highest levels of energy? During their late teens and early twenties – when they are courting. So with time and boundless energy their romance flourishes. They go out on dates five nights a week. Stay up talking till 2 a.m. Schedule breakfast meetings before dawn so they can watch the sunrise. Many college couples do what we did. As soon as the young man's Friday afternoon class ends, he jumps in his car and drives fourteen hours to his girlfriend's college, where he spends a day and a half with her before driving back to his campus for his Monday morning class. The next weekend she visits him.

But few couples can maintain that pace over the long haul. During the coming years their energy levels seem to plummet. One beautiful summer evening (the kind they used to think was created for romance), after they put the kids to bed at 8 p.m., the young wife halfheartedly suggests they take a walk around the block.

'Are you kidding?' says her weary husband. 'I feel like I'm dead on my feet already, and I have to be at the office at 6 a.m.'

'Yeah, I know. I feel the same way, and the baby will probably be up again in a few hours. Maybe some other time.'

What really complicates things is that at the same time their energy drops, their responsibilities skyrocket. Career. Kids. Car pools. The PTA. The handyman special they call a house. In-law challenges. Church involvement. Community service. And then they look in the mirror and notice that their bodies need a little attention, so they try to squeeze in some exercise.

In addition to increased responsibility and time commitments, there is often an increased financial burden. During courtship many young people live with parents or roommates and have minimal living expenses. So they have plenty of excess money to spend on dates. One young man told us about renting a tux to wear to take his girlfriend out for dinner – just for fun. We thought, *Wait till that guy gets married. Wait till he's making house payments and buying cars and furniture. And wait till he's raising kids.* Kids are fun, but they are costly little critters. His wife is going to suggest a quiet, get-away dinner, and he is going to break his arm patting himself on the back for wearing a three-year-old sports jacket. His tux days are going to seem like a lifetime away. Who thinks about long-stemmed roses and romantic dinners when you need a crib, a lawn mower, and a new roof?

As the years pass, life gets more and more complicated. What usually takes the brunt of all the madness? Marriage. *He can wait. She will understand. We'll attend to the marriage later, when we have more time and more energy and more creativity and more money.*

But that seldom happens. Why? Because while all of these complicating factors are entering the marriage picture, there is something even more sinister going on beneath the surface of too many marriages. We have discovered that many marriages that are short on romance have arrived at that unpleasant spot via a common route. Though the coming illustration focuses primarily on a husband's error in judgment, more and more wives are making the same mistake.

Top Priority

The journey begins like this. A young man identifies the woman he wants to marry and begins the business of serious courtship. Time and money are no object, so he throws vast amounts of energy and creativity into the pursuit. He gives gifts, sends cards, writes poems, delivers flowers, plans romantic dinners in elegant restaurants, takes long walks on sandy beaches, enjoys leisurely drives on country roads, and loiters in front of glittering jewellery store windows. He is on a mission. He has a worthy goal. He is motivated. He lets nothing stand in the way of winning the woman of his dreams. She becomes his top priority, and he will not rest until she is his.

He is smitten and he wants her to know it. He rearranges his busy schedule to spend every possible minute with her. He compliments her warmly. He sings her praises to friends and family. He talks about her constantly. And very slowly he begins to wear her down.

That's right, wear her down. You see, she was a little suspicious at first. He was obviously in hot pursuit, but what exactly did that mean? What was he after? Did he want a cheap thrill or a lasting relationship? A female trophy or a wife he could treasure? She knows the dangers because she has been hurt before. So she wisely guards her heart and maintains her distance. She observes, waits, and analyses. Can this guy be trusted? Or will he dash her dreams six months after the wedding? She has heard the horror stories, and doesn't intend to provide the plot for another one.

Meanwhile, the diligent young man showers her with attention, affection and appreciation. He calls her four times a day, fills her mailbox with declarations of love, and buys her sentimental gifts and exotic perfumes. The weekends are wall-to-wall recreation and romance: dinners, movies, plays, parties. And now – the offer of a diamond ring.

Almost against her will, she feels loved. She feels safe and secure and treasured and prized and wanted. She begins to trust him. She begins to believe that it will last. In fact, she lets herself believe that it will keep getting better and better, and that marriage will open the door to a future of unimagined joy.

Finally, the last bridge of doubt is crossed and she says, 'Yes, yes, I will marry you. You have proven beyond a shadow of doubt that you love me. You have courted me, romanced me, made me feel special and important and treasured. You have convinced me that I am at the top of your priority list. You have won my heart. I will marry you!'

So the wedding date is set, the ceremony is carefully planned, and the honeymoon is arranged. It all comes off in storybook style. The newly married couple move into their cosy studio apartment and the young wife settles into the realities of everyday married life, revelling in the knowledge that she made a wise and wonderful choice for a lifetime partner.

I Got That Job Done!

And then it happens. Her husband does a terrible, horrible, awful, unthinkable, rotten, reprehensible thing. Oh, he doesn't realize he is doing anything wrong. But he does it, nonetheless, and deeply wounds his sincere, trusting wife.

What does he do? He shifts gear. He readjusts his focus. He figures that now that he got the 'marriage job' done it is time to move on to another objective. He faced one chal-lenge and beat it; now it is time to face another one. So without giving one thought to how this is going to impact his wife, he calmly rearranges his priorities, reapportions his energies, and launches out on his next mission, most likely in the marketplace.

There is no malice in his decision. In fact, he is probably not even aware that he is making the shift. If questioned about his love for his wife, he would deny that it has faltered in the least. He loves her as much as he did the day he married her. He is simply doing what he has been conditioned to do.

It goes all the way back to childhood. Dad assigns the little guy a list of responsibilities and says, 'Now, you do this chore, and when you complete it satisfactorily, then you move on to the next chore, and you continue till you work your way down the list.' So the little guy does exactly as he is told. He completes one chore, then shifts his focus to the next one. When he gets older and becomes involved in athletics, he learns quickly how the system works. First there are the tryouts; then the practices and the games; finally, the tournaments and the award banquets. Then you put that uniform away, and three weeks later you shift your focus to the next sport.

It is the same in the marketplace. He receives an assignment from his manager and is told to work on it, complete it, and then present it. After he does that, he packs up and moves to the next assignment. This *modus operandi*, this task-oriented approach, becomes a way of life for many men, and it extends right into their relational lives. Marriage seems to fit the pattern perfectly. They pour their efforts into courtship, get the marriage job done, and attend the award banquet – the honeymoon. Then they move on to the next job, the next task, the next challenge.

Not all men do this, of course. But it is not uncommon. Many men are raised this way, and without giving it a moment's thought, they function this way. It comes naturally for them and makes perfect sense. 'Yeah,' a man says, 'I do operate that way. What's the big deal? It's interesting, but far from earth-shattering.'

A Nightmare Come True

Unfortunately, it *is* earth-shattering to the unsuspecting, trusting woman he married. Throughout the courtship she had been leery. She had questioned and analysed. But he had been so tenacious, so convincing. Finally, she gave in. She let herself feel treasured. And now, just as she sits poised with pen in hand, preparing to write the story on wedded bliss, her husband closes the book so he can focus on a new agenda. He wants to make a buck or two. Or climb a rung or two. Or build a church or two. And he works so hard he no longer has the time or energy for love letters or long walks or candlelight dinners or flowers or phone calls or back rubs or three-hour conversations about building a life together. Those were front-burner issues back when he was trying to get the marriage job done, but now it's done. To complicate matters, he convinces himself that the best way to show love for his wife is to provide well for her. So, with even greater abandon, he throws himself into his work.

The young wife is devastated. Her worst nightmare is coming true. She views his refocus of attention as evidence of personal rejection. 'I guarded my heart for two and a half years,' she cries. 'And then I let myself be fooled. I bought hook, line, and sinker into all the wining, dining, and courting. And now here I sit. I was duped. Set up. How could I have been so stupid?'

Sometimes the husband's behaviour wipes out his wife's self-esteem. Sometimes it just makes her angry. Either way, it convinces her that she married the wrong man.

We recently attended a small conference with a number of couples in the fifty- to sixty-year age range. We observed that many of the men were unusually attentive towards their wives. Because we were in the midst of working on this book, we asked them why. Almost without exception, the men said, 'This is my second wife. During my first marriage

I was too preoccupied with climbing the corporate ladder to pay attention to my wife. I hurt her deeply for many years, and finally she couldn't take it anymore. Now I'm doing things differently. I may have forfeited my first wife, but I'm not going to foul things up again.'

Most men don't intend to hurt their wives. They do what they do without thinking. And, as we mentioned earlier, husbands aren't the only ones who fall into this pattern. The unprecedented entrance of women into the marketplace has put wives at equal risk when it comes to refocusing their energies and neglecting romance. In many marriages nowadays, both spouses make the destructive shift. A young couple we know were best friends all through high school, dated happily throughout college, and married with the total blessing of family and friends. But five years into marriage they sat across from one another on their living room floor, weeping over the lack of feeling in their marriage. They weren't spiritually incompatible. They hadn't lost respect for one another. They didn't have serious temperament clashes or poor conflict resolution skills. They had simply poured themselves into their careers and neglected to treasure one another.

While some people let their careers get in the way of romance, others get sidetracked by parenting. They get so caught up in child-rearing responsibilities that they forget they are husbands and wives first, parents second. In attempting to give their best to their children, they fail to give them what they need most: a happily married mum and dad.

Wouldn't It Be Nice...

'How are things going at home?'
    'How are you and your wife getting along?'
    'How is your relationship with your husband?'
    Too often the responses to such questions reveal a less-than-happy state of affairs.

'Well, uh, not bad, tolerable. You know how it goes.'

'Oh, all right. I suppose it could be better.'

'You asked me at a bad time.'

Wouldn't it be nice if more couples could answer those questions like this:

'We're having a great time. Our marriage is better than ever.'

'I'm nuts about my wife. I love being with her.'

'I'm crazy about my husband. We have so much fun together.'

Wouldn't it be nice to see more husbands and wives finding great delight in one another? And developing soul companionship with one another? And deepening their lifelong commitments to one another? Wouldn't it be nice to see more couples modelling a tremendous marriage so their kids will know what to aim for when they get married? Wouldn't it be nice to see romance taking its rightful place in marriage?

Some people think that the only way to get romance back in their marriage is to get into a different marriage. But many people who opt out of a romanceless marriage find themselves, two or three years later, in another romanceless marriage. They thought they needed a new partner, but what they really needed was a new pattern of relating and expressing love. They thought they needed a new marriage, but what they really needed was a new motivation for rekindling their old one.

Our Journey Back

B   One thing that really bothered me during the early years of our marriage was that Lynne kept pushing to build a great marriage. She wanted our marriage to be out of the ordinary. She had lofty goals regarding oneness and companionship and romance. She was committed to pursuing an ideal marriage.

I, like many people, was content with a mediocre marriage. Five on a ten scale was fine with me. I loved Lynne and was committed to the institution of marriage, but I couldn't see being preoccupied with marriage when there were so many other things to be concerned about. I was busy building a church. I was busy developing a staff. I was busy leading people to Christ. I was busy trying to make the house payment. I was busy trying to be a great father to my kids. I was busy, I tell you! I couldn't figure out why Lynne was so bound and determined to get such lofty and time-consuming goals for our relationship. Though I never verbally condemned her expectations, I made my position known in a thousand nonverbal ways. I was more than willing to settle for average.

I tried to convince myself that it was a time problem, that I didn't have enough hours in my day to build a great marriage. But it was really a motivation problem. I did not have an inner drive to build my marriage.

At sixteen, when I became a Christian, I knew that Jesus Christ had done for me what I couldn't do for myself — purchased my eternal salvation. And I was determined to express my gratitude by obeying His commandments and serving Him diligently. One of the first verses I memorized was Colossians 3:23, 'Whatever you do, work at it with all your heart, as working for the Lord, not for men.'

I knew I fell far short, but I was sincere and kept striving. I nurtured my daily walk with Jesus Christ wholeheartedly. I devoted myself to my ministry wholeheartedly. I developed and used my spiritual gifts wholeheartedly. I pursued purity and love in my friendships wholeheartedly. I committed myself to fatherhood wholeheartedly.

But in my relationship with my wife, I was halfhearted. I don't remember why. Maybe I didn't know how to be wholehearted in marriage. Maybe I was overwhelmed by the challenge. Maybe I truly thought a mediocre marriage was all God had in mind for us. For whatever the reason, I applied a different standard to marriage.

In nearly every other area of my life I was disciplined and goal oriented, and I sought to please and honour God. But in my marriage I was undisciplined, I had established low goals, and I failed to view marital growth as a matter of obedience. As a result, I saw examples of divine intervention and supernatural blessing in every area of my life except my relationship with Lynne.

Eventually the contrast between what was happening in my marriage and what was happening in the rest of my life – and the chastising words of some close friends who observed my behaviour towards Lynne – kicked some sense into me. I finally took off the marital blinders and noticed what the Bible had to say to husbands. In Ephesians 5:25, Paul tells husbands to 'treasure your wives'. A Greek verb study revealed that the present imperative tense was used in this verse. So a more accurate translation would be: 'Husbands, *keep on treasuring* your wives.' That verse hit me like a bulldozer. I wasn't treasuring Lynne. I had shifted gears with the best of 'em. I had gotten the marriage job done and moved on to new challenges. I was blatantly violating God's command.

First Peter 3:7 tells husbands to 'be considerate as you live with your wives, and treat them with respect'. I wasn't doing that. I wasn't being sensitive towards Lynne. I wasn't showing her courtesy or honour or respect. At least not wholeheatedly.

I don't know why I had been so blind before, but when I finally started seeing clearly, I decided to do something about it. I have to confess that I was not at that point motivated by my feelings for Lynne. Though I was committed to her and to our marriage, my gear-shifting routine had wounded her so deeply that she had become hostile and cold. Because I didn't understand what had caused her to become that way, I responded with anger and impatience and frustration. So the tension between us was high, the warmth was low, and there was little on a feeling level to motivate me to move towards her.

What did motivate me was the sudden realization that being totally devoted to my wife – and to rekindling our marriage – was part of my commitment to God.

Since the day I became a Christian I have longed to hear God say someday, 'Well done, Bill. You have served Me faithfully. You have obeyed Me conscientiously. You have pleased Me in your personal walk with Me, in your ministry, in your teaching, in your financial management, in your parenting, in your friendships, in how you have treated your body. Well done. Thank you for trusting Me. Thank you for standing strong for Me.'

Now I wanted to add my marriage to the list. I wanted to be able to hear someday, 'Well done, Bill. You have been a godly husband. You kept on treasuring your wife.' So I vowed to become devoted to Lynne, to begin treasuring her the way I was supposed to. And I promised to do it even if she didn't make a reciprocal commitment.

As it turned out, that was a good thing. By the time I made this covenant with God, it was almost too late for Lynne. She had been so wounded by my neglect that she responded to my dramatic turnaround with little more than indifference for nearly two years. That was extremely frustrating for me, but it did not undermine my commitment to wholeheartedness, because my motivation was not centred on Lynne's response. I learned that God is faithful to give us the strength and courage we need to make the changes required by obedience. And my obedience freed us to take the long journey back to romance.

Healthy Options

And it *was* a long journey. Closing the book on romance had done so much damage to our relationship that we were beyond the help of a quick cure. In retrospect, however, we see ways that we could have minimized the damage and shortened the healing process.

L

Early in our marriage I tried to call for help and express my hurt. I tried to tell Bill that I felt neglected, like the last item on his priority list, and that I sensed us drifting apart. But he didn't see it. He thought I was being unreasonable. So he refused to change.

Eventually my hurt turned to anger, and I alternated between sullen withdrawal and hateful outbursts. Both reactions drove Bill deeper into his work and further away from romance. Why, he asked himself, should he come home to a wife who was detached one day, and openly antagonistic the next? In his work, he was successful and productive; he received affirmation; he spent his days with pleasant people. At home, he felt judged and condemned, and daily faced an unhappy wife. Had he not been convicted by the Word of God, he would probably never have reopened the book on romance and made marriage the priority it is supposed to be.

Bill was wrong to 'get the marriage job done' and move on. But I was wrong to let my hurt turn to anger, and exacerbate the problem. I should have modified my approach so I wouldn't have 'sinned in my anger'.

First, I should have expressed my hurt more assertively. I should have gone back to Bill again and again, using the conflict resolution techniques described in chapter 3, and repeated to him how I felt. I gave up too easily on the positive forms of communication and slipped too quickly into destructive patterns that drove us farther apart.

Of course, it is easy to say in retrospect what I should have done. In reality, asserting myself was no small task because my self-esteem had been severely damaged by Bill's shift. I no longer trusted my own insights. I was unsure of my feelings and opinions. In addition to that, because Bill was in the ministry, asking him to spend more time and energy on me meant that he would have less to devote to 'God's work'. That was a pretty heavy demand for a young wife to make.

I realize now that I should have talked with trusted friends who could have given me an accurate perspective on what was happening in our marriage. I needed objective outsiders who could affirm my position and give me the confidence to speak up, and also remind me of the dangers of holding back and allowing my hurt to turn to anger.

My next step, if communicating more assertively didn't help, should have been to suggest that Bill and I meet together with another couple. If Bill couldn't hear what I was saying, or if I was letting anger sabotage the process, perhaps our third-party friends could have moderated the communication process and facilitated understanding.

If that option didn't help, I should have suggested marriage counselling. If Bill refused to go, I should have gone to a counsellor myself. I should have talked with someone who could have helped me process the hurt before it poisoned our relationship, and could have helped me formulate a workable plan of action or, as a last resort, an ultimatum.

An ultimatum? That's right. An ultimatum that would have caught Bill's attention. That would have forced action. That would have said, 'I love you, but I can't take this any more.'

A short period of separation would have been one possible ultimatum. We have often wondered what effect a separation early in our marriage, monitored by a wise Christian counsellor, would have had on the course of our relationship. It would have been traumatic, indeed, but it may well have broken a hurtful pattern that plagued us for years, minimized the damage done to our relationship, and significantly shortened the period of healing.

Seldom is one spouse responsible for ending the story of a romance. While one may be responsible for turning the page, the other's reaction may be what finally closes the book. To rewrite the story, both need to admit their sin, seek forgiveness, and adopt a new plan for the future.

The Place to Start

What about you? Have you shifted gears and wounded your spouse? Have you become too preoccupied with competing demands? Have you allowed fatigue or financial problems or kids to drain the romance out of your marriage? Have you allowed the feelings to fade? Have you given up? Have you let hurt turn to anger? Have you concluded that you married the wrong person? Are you weary of the work of marriage? Do you lack the motivation to try again?

Maybe you need a private encounter with God. Maybe you need to take the blinders off and look at what Scripture says about marriage. Maybe you need to get down on your knees and commit yourself to becoming a wholehearted marriage partner. Maybe you need to say, 'Forget what everybody else does. Forget what I've done in the past. Lord, out of gratitude for what You have done for me I want to obey You in every area of my life, including my marriage. I am going to begin treasuring my spouse. I am going to begin respecting my spouse. I am going to bring the romance back to my marriage.'

If you are feeling overwhelmed by the challenge, please don't lose hope. God can help you rekindle your marriage. He offers you His motivation, His wisdom, His power, His encouragement, and His supernatural intervention. Ephesians 3:20 tells us that God 'is able to do immeasurably more than all we ask or imagine'.

But it's our move. We have to ask Him. We have to commit ourselves to obedience. Then God can bring the surprises. Not overnight. Not without work and pain and honest communication. But when His supernatural intervention comes to bear on our efforts, romance can be rekindled.

In the next chapter we want to look beyond the motivation to some of the practical mechanics of rebuilding romance.

Fanning the Flames
of Marriage

L It was a Wednesday in May, 1989. At 10 p.m., following our
midweek church service, we loaded our luggage into our car
and began a night-time journey to a destination I did not
know. It was our fifteenth wedding anniversary and Bill had
made all the arrangements, including a baby-sitter for the kids.
All I had to do was pack according to his careful instructions.

After two hours on the road we stopped at an all-night
restaurant and had dessert. It was a truckstop that had marked
the halfway point when we used to drive from Kalamazoo to
Chicago during our dating years. Sometimes we made the trip
to buy produce at Chicago's Water Street Market for Bill's
dad. Other times Bill drove me back to college or picked me
up for a weekend break. Sitting there eating hot apple pie, we
reminisced about those years. We talked about how much we
had enjoyed those drives. About the nonstop talk that had
filled the eight-hour round trips. And about how we had hated
seeing the Kalamazoo exit on the way back because it signalled
our return to real life and our respective homes. By the time
we resumed our journey, we felt like those dating kids again.
Only this time we didn't have to meet a midnight curfew.

When we took the I-96 cutoff I guessed where we were
headed, and I was right. Within an hour we were walking on
the South Haven beach where we had walked on our first

official date in 1969. There was the same concrete breaker upon which we had sat. The same lighthouse under which we had talked. The same moon whose beauty we had admired.

It was 3 a.m. We sat on the beach, digging our toes into the sand, watching the moonlit waves shimmy up the sodden bank. With each wave came a memory that crashed into our consciousness. A memory of a slammed door and a cancelled courtship. Of making up, and of a carnival wedding. A memory of joy surrounding a baby's birth, and of tears shed in a cracker-box home. Of ministry moments that boggled our minds, and of a heartrending ride in a blue Suburban. Memories of a perfect vacation, of criticism and judgment, of celebrating uniqueness. Memories of feelings smothered by pain, and of a rekindled romance.

We were seventeen when we first sat together on that Lake Michigan beach – and naive. We foresaw only sunny days. By thirty-seven our naivete had been battered and finally destroyed by rainstorms and lightning and gale-force winds. But while our naivete had not survived, we had. We had come face to face with reality and we had stared it down. We had persevered and worked hard and won. And we sat on that beach stronger and more mature and more tolerant and more in love than ever.

Can a battered romance be rebuilt? Can the smouldering embers of dying feelings be refuelled? We think they can be. We think that the love that drew a couple together in courtship can be recaptured and sustained, in spite of disappointments and setbacks and stormy weather. In this chapter we want to give some practical suggestions for doing just that.

Talk, Talk, Talk

Feelings grow best out of conversation, so that is where we want to start. Couples must devote themselves to talking –

about anything, everything, important things, mundane things, pleasant things, disturbing things. Romance begins with knowledge of one another, and the key to knowledge is open, honest, consistent communication.

Our teenage daughter has a new boyfriend. Recently she spent a Saturday afternoon with him. They ran a few errands, then sat on a picnic table in a forest preserve and talked. 'You talked?' we asked. 'All afternoon? About what?'

'You know. About everything. About school and church and our friends. About what we like and don't like. About what we're going to do this summer. About our goals. About college. About what makes us mad or happy. About you guys! It was wonderful.'

Do you remember when there weren't enough hours in the day to contain your conversations? Do you remember how close you felt? How tuned in you were to each other?

Is it any wonder we lose the warmth in our relationships when we only talk on the run, when we leave each other memos on the kitchen table and messages on the answering machine? Too often spouses don't feel for one another any more because they don't know one another any more. They don't know each other's fears or dreams or goals or disappointments or plans. They don't know what goes on during each other's day. They aren't aware of the joys, the stresses, the responsibilities, the successes that fill their spouse's world.

Husbands and wives ought to find comfort in one another's presence. Their marriage should be a place of refuge. There ought to be an underlying sense that 'it's you and me against the world'. But it will never be that way unless spouses make time for in-depth communication on a regular basis. That is why a weekly date outside the home is so important. And why we need to take advantage of every opportunity to 'catch up' on what is going on with our spouses. An after-dinner conversation while the kids clear the table, or an evening walk around the block, or even an afternoon telephone call to find out what the doctor said or how things went at the meeting can keep spouses informed and build on the sense of unity and caring established during more lengthy and significant conversations.

If the romance in your marriage has received a near-deadly blow, your conversations will undoubtedly have to begin by focusing on hidden hostilities. If you are like us, you are probably tempted to bypass this and move to more pleasant conversations. 'The past is past,' you say. 'Let's forget it and move into the future.' But that won't work. Underground hurts will determine even our most earnest attempts to rebuild romance, and you will end up more frustrated than when you started.

'I know you didn't intend to hurt me, but you did. I felt put down and rejected every time you said you were too busy to spend time with me.' With those words, a friend of ours hoped to release once and for all the anger she felt towards her previously overscheduled husband. Because her husband was sincerely apologetic and committed to reopening the book on romance, she assumed she was free to focus on the future. But a short time later, she was again bursting with anger. 'Do you realize what it was like to feel like the last item on your priority list? Do you realize how awful that was?'

That woman learned something very important about hidden hostilities: it is unrealistic to expect negative emotions that have built up over a number of years to dissipate in one conversation. People who have been deeply hurt need to give themselves the freedom to constructively express their hurt over and over again, if necessary. Those who caused the pain need to listen patiently, understanding that while working through past hurts can be painful and sometimes seem counterproductive, it is *essential* to rebuilding romance.

What complicates the process is that usually both spouses have caused hurt and received it. Sometimes a counsellor can help sort through the confusion and assist spouses in asserting their own pain, while at the same time being sensitive to the other's pain. Again, it is tempting to jump over this step. But taking a responsible approach to past hurts, even if that means devoting six months or a year to counselling, will make the difference between smouldering embers and a roaring bonfire.

After you face up to past hurts and work through them, you can protect your new sense of unity and warmth by dealing with new conflicts as they arise. Planning frequent peace talks will clear the air and keep hurts from going underground again. Nothing destroys romance like an edge of anger. As the old adage says, it's no fun to hug a porcupine.

Court Creatively

After you get rid of hidden hostilities and learn what it means to talk again, you can begin to court creatively. Most couples put the wedding gifts away and their courting days behind them. But if you want to rebuild romance you need to court again.

Fortunately, courting is like riding a bike; you may get a little rusty, but you never forget how. So take a few minutes over lunch and write a simple note to your spouse. 'I was just thinking about you and wanted to tell you I love you.' 'If I had it to do over again, I'd marry you in a minute. I'm excited about what the future will bring.' Then put it in the mail. Imagine how your spouse will feel, expecting a list of chores you want done, and finding a love note instead.

Or you might consider calling your spouse during the day for no reason. 'Hi. How are you? I was just wondering how your day was going.' It means so much to a husband or wife to know that their spouse was thinking about them – and took the time to say it.

L

I know how busy Bill is when he is at the office, and he knows how hectic my day can be. So taking a few minutes to call and 'check in' says something to both of us. It tells me that Bill cares more about me than the papers stacked on his desk and the calls he has to return. It tells him that the article I'm working on or the tasks that fill my day are not as important to me as he is.

Nonsexual touching is another important part of courting. If your first response to that sentence is that it is nonsense, it is no wonder the romance has drained out of your marriage. As important as sexual touch is – and we will talk about it later – warm, loving, nonsexual touch is every bit as essential to a romance-filled marriage.

Too many spouses do little more than give each other a obligatory kiss when they part ways in the morning and then repeat the routine when they greet one another at night. Their lips touch, but they barely even know it. It has become an involuntary response. Adding a little variety to touching can take it out of the autopilot realm and put the feeling back in it. When you take an after-dinner walk, reach down and grab your spouse's hand – and think about what you are doing. Let your clasped hands symbolize the lifetime commitment you have made to one another. While your spouse reads the paper, bend down and gently rub his or her neck; think of it as a comforting act of tenderness, as a way to ease the stress of a busy day. While you watch the night-time news, put your arm around your spouse and say with that gesture, 'I'm so glad we had another day to share together.' An obligatory kiss is barely noticed. But touch that is backed by feeling is a match that can reignite a dying flame.

Flowers still spell romance. But don't just buy the daily special. Think back to your dating days. Did your spouse have a favourite flower? Was there a special occasion marked by a red rose? Do you recall a romantic evening complete with a beautiful corsage? Get creative. On your way to dinner, present your wife with a purple orchid like the one she wore to the prom. Buy a bouquet of sweetheart roses in honour of the flowers she carried on your wedding day.

If flowers never earned a place in your memory bank, don't despair. Ask your wife what kind she likes. Chances are she won't remember – it's been so long since it mattered – but give her time. Once the shock wears off and her senses return, she will describe the perfect bouquet. Ordering precisely what she describes will tell her that her preferences, her desires, her tastes matter to you. It will say, 'I still treasure you.'

Dating is another important part of courting. Watching our daughter prepare for a date is like watching the planning of a national event. First come the numerous phone calls to decide when to schedule the event. Then another slew of calls to discuss where to go for the event. Finally, there is a full-scale fashion show to determine what to wear to the event. Sadly, such enthusiasm wanes over the years. For many married couples, going out on a date is barely an event at all. They give it little thought or discussion ahead of time and squeeze it between 'more important' commitments, go wherever the car takes them, and never consider dressing up 'just for each other'. No wonder their evenings out add little spark to their relationship.

We have friends who always discuss their Friday night date during dinner on the previous Monday. They look through the entertainment section of the Sunday newspaper, consider various options, then decide together what they want to do. Then they have all week to anticipate their plans and remind each other in notes or calls that 'We're going to have a great time on Friday night,' or 'It's been a long week, but we'll be able to celebrate soon.' They each make the evening more special by wearing clothes the other particularly likes. 'I love it,' says the wife, 'when my husband walks out of the bedroom looking great in something he knows I like. It makes me feel like it's a real "date", the kind we enjoyed when we first met and were trying to catch each other's eye. It also tells me that my husband still thinks I'm worth "looking good for". That means a lot to me!'

Another aspect of courting creatively is serving one another. During high school a young man carries his girlfriend's books and she makes him chocolate chip cookies. In college he hauls her suitcases and she types his term paper. During engagement he fixes her car and she does his laundry. (Or vice versa.) But six months after the wedding, they retire their sevant's uniforms. Suddenly it's every man for himself; every woman for herself. They hide the uniforms in the back of the hallway closet, and with them the warm feelings that service engenders. If a husband and wife want to heat up those feelings again, they need to squeeze themselves back into those uniforms, blow the dust off the shoulders, and get back to serving. Discovering and joyfully offering small acts of service that bring special delight to a spouse is a great way to change the tone of a relationship.

B

After fifteen years of driving high-mileage, boat-sized, family vehicles, Lynne made a switch to a new, down-sized, red Toyota that she loves. It represents a rite of passage for her, a delightful freedom from hauling cribs and car seats and bicycles and basketball teams. One way I have found to serve her is to make sure her little car is never less than sparkling. I blow the budget on Turtle Wax and Armor All, but it's worth it to see the smile on her face when she slides behind the wheel of an immaculate car.

In spite of the influence of the women's movement, women still tend to end up doing more than their share of mundane, time-consuming, exhausting, thankless household tasks. One way for husbands to get beyond cheap talk is to cheerfully and voluntarily assume more of these responsibilities. During the early years of our marriage I flagrantly violated this principle. Since then I have learned that planning special activities for the kids, or doing the dishes, or putting away the groceries, or vacuuming the living room, or making travel arrangements, or stopping at the dry cleaners are essential though neglected parts of romance.

Creative courting also includes inspiring our spouses. Do you remember how often you used to cheer each other on when you were dating? 'You have so much potential!' 'You're going to be a great lawyer someday.' 'You can succeed at whatever you choose.' 'You belong on the stage; you played that role perfectly.' 'I'll stand by you no matter what.' 'I can't wait to see you soar.' 'That was great how you caught that line drive this afternoon.' 'You have tremendous gifts and abilities.' 'I'm so proud of you.' But now that you've settled into life's routines, do you even pay attention to what your spouse is doing? Do you comment on accomplishments or encourage after failures? Are you the biggest cheerleader your spouse has?

When we started our church we took a door-to-door survey of our community. We asked people who didn't regularly attend church what there was about church that drove them away. The most common complaint was that church services were dull, repetitive, routine and predictable. Unfortunately, that same complaint can be made of many marriages. That is why we talk about courting creatively. While boredom puts both church members and spouses to sleep, creativity has a powerful way of jarring people awake and exciting their emotions. Creativity tells a spouse that rebuilding romance is important to you. It is worthy of your time, your thought, your energy. It is a priority. After years of neglect, that is often the message a spouse most needs to hear. It is the jump-start that can get damaged feelings working again.

Language of Love

Although we offered a few specific suggestions about courting creatively, only you can determine the best way to court your spouse. Why? Because every husband and every wife is different and has different ways of giving and receiving love. In order to court your spouse meaningfully, you need to determine which is his or her preferred *language of love*.

For some people touch is the primary language of love. Their spouse can say 'I love you' twenty times a day and prove it through countless actions of kindness, but without an embrace or a kiss or a squeeze they won't *feel* loved.

Other people need to hear verbal expressions of love. They need to hear in concrete terms why their spouse loves them. 'I'm glad I married you because...' assures them that their spouse recognizes and appreciates their individuality.

Service is what makes some people feel most loved. They respond best to affection that is revealed in practical terms: cooking a meal, mowing the lawn, repairing a tap, running an errand, helping with a distasteful chore. These people see acts of service as indicative of what is in their spouse's heart.

Gifts make other people feel loved – not because of the cost involved, but because of the personal attention and thought that goes into them. These people enjoy – even need – tangible reminders of their spouse's love.

Some people feel loved when their spouse offers them opportunities for pleasure or self-improvement. They appreciate a spouse who says, 'I heard of a seminar I think you would enjoy. Why don't you take it?' That convinces them that their spouse cares about the things that are important to them.

Spending time together makes other people feel loved. They don't care particularly what they and their spouses do, as long as they are together. Having their husband or wife commit uninterrupted blocks of time to them assures them they are top priority.

Do you know which language of love is important to your spouse?

B

For years I assumed that the best way to convince Lynne that I loved her was to remind her repeatedly why I had married her. 'I really appreciate your spirituality,' I'd tell her, 'and your intelligence and your conscientiousness. I respect your character, and I think you'll make a great mother someday.' I was sure that would make her feel loved.

But it didn't. She appreciated it, but it wasn't enough to convince her of my love. She needed to receive love through the language of touch; she needed lots of physical affection. She also needed my time. She needed me to take the initiative in setting aside quiet hours on a regular basis when we could be together. For years, I gave her neither.

Why did I assume that verbal expressions of love would do the job? Because that was the love language I preferred. It made me feel great when Lynne told me she was proud of something I had done or that she loved a certain aspect of my character or personality. I didn't need her to hug me or squeeze my hand or spend large blocks of time with me, as much as I needed her to build me up with her words. I needed to know she loved and respected the unique qualities that made me *me*. So I assumed that was all she needed.

Making assumptions about the language of love our spouse prefers often leads to disappointment, and sometimes even to misunderstanding.

L

Another way Bill showed love to me was by providing me with opportunities – more than I could possibly take advantage of. He was always saying, 'You should take that writing assignment. You would do a superb job.' Or, 'That is a great speaking opportunity. You would really minister to those women.' Or, 'You should join me on this trip. You would have fun and meet lots of interesting people.' Or, 'Why don't you sign up for a wilderness survival weekend? You would learn so much.'

On one hand, I appreciated the confidence he seemed to have in my abilities. On the other hand, it seemed that he wasn't satisfied with me the way I was. He was always pushing me to do more, accomplish more, relate more, learn more. And taking advantage of even a fraction of the opportunities he threw my way filled my time to overflowing and created a high level of stress.

When I finally told him how I felt, he was shocked. 'I get a kick out of providing opportunities for the people I love,' he said. 'I wasn't trying to "push" you.'

Bill is a wonderful leader, friend, and father because he delights in opening doors of opportunity for those around him. That's his most comfortable and natural way of expressing love. When I came to understand that, I began to appreciate the opportunities he provided and began to feel loved instead of 'pushed'. I was free to respond to those that interested me and say 'No thanks' to the rest.

Husbands and wives need to pinpoint their own and their spouse's preferred languages of love, and then negotiate a way to make sure they both receive love in the language they can understand. That often requires flexibility, sensitivity, and a willingness to grow in areas where we may be weak.

L

As mentioned earlier, Bill hears love best when it's expressed in verbal terms. He needs me to tell him that I love him – and tell him why in creative, meaningful, specific terms. Unfortunately, verbal expression is not my strong suit. I have had to remind myself daily that Bill needs my words, just as he has had to remind himself daily that I need physical affection. And when either of us gets careless or forgetful, the other has to put pride aside and be vulnerable enough to say, 'I'm not feeling very loved. Would you please say it again in terms I can understand.'

Focus on the Fun Side

If you want to rekindle romance, you should commit yourself to meaningful conversation, court creatively, learn one another's language of love, and now, start to have some fun again.

It may help to think back to your dating years and try to recapture some of the fun moments you shared then. Brush up on your tennis skills. Go to an afternoon baseball game. Spend a Saturday at the beach. Set up a volleyball net in the backyard. Go to a concert. Plan a picnic. Ride bikes through the country. Walk through an art gallery. Go to a silly movie. Roast marshmallows over a bonfire.

It is so easy for life to get too serious. Couples talk about money and kids, about jobs and responsibilities, about fears and old age. And they forget what it means to laugh and to play and to feel like kids again.

Even the best marriages take a tremendous amount of work. If there is no fun to balance out the work, even the most earnest spouses begin to lose motivation and energy. And the more challenging a marriage is, the more important fun is. We have learned that mutually enjoyable, fun experiences can help heal tender wounds and become a bridge across frustrating differences.

We enjoy attending cultural events together, reading the same books and comparing insights, and spending time with mutual friends. But our most enjoyable activities tend to centre around sports. We both love sailing and water skiing, hiking and snow skiing, and running and working out together. Because of our differences, we were delighted to discover these common interests and deliberately plan many marital and family occasions around these mutual activities. If we want to plan a weekend getaway that is a 'sure thing' we'll go where there are plenty of walking trails or a lake with rental sailboats. We have learned that a healthy shot of fun can carry us through a lot of hard work, so we make no apology for scheduling fun as often as we can.

Several years ago we talked with a Christian man who had committed adultery. Putting a loving hand on our shoulders, he begged us to commit ourselves to having fun in our marriage. 'I have always loved my wife,' he said. 'But our relationship became businesslike. We poured our energy into our jobs, raising our children, helping in the community, and serving together in our church, but we didn't take time to have fun together. So, when someone came along and offered me laughter and lightheartedness, a respite from all the work and responsibility, I was a sitting duck. I fell for the promise of a little fun. How I wish my wife and I had taken the time to play.'

How is the fun factor in your marriage? If it needs a boost, begin to experiment. Schedule a variety of activities and see which ones you like. Take a class together and see if you can discover a new interest. Ask other couples for ideas. Look in the entertainment section of your local newspaper. Be open-minded. Be bold. Try new things. Fun and laughter have a wonderful way of breaking down inhibitions, generating warmth, and leading to...

Even More Fun

If you have been wondering when we were going to get around to talking about sex, you need wonder no longer. We have waited till the end of the chapter to discuss it because we have learned that mutually satisfying sex starts with communication, creative courting, meaningful expressions of love, and shared fun. The actual act of sex is the culmination of a series of encounters that set the tone and create the desire for total, loving, physical intimacy.

We believe sex should be the ultimate fun activity a couple shares. Unfortunately, for many couples, including us during the early years of our marriage, sex provides more frustration than fun. A small percentage of couples suffer from true sexual dysfunctions of either physical or psychological origins. We encourage them to consult a doctor or a counsellor. Applying simplistic answers to their complex problems would only increase their frustration.

Even aside from sexual dysfunctions, human sexuality is very complex and affected by a myriad of personal and relational factors. Obviously we cannot, in a few short pages, look in depth at such a broad subject. We have found, however, that many couples in the process of rebuilding romance can benefit from a slight shift in attitude or from a few fresh ideas regarding sexual experience. That's what we needed.

Fun for Whom?

Like many young married couples, we read our share of books about sex. We easily dismissed those authors who viewed sexual intercourse solely as a means of procreation, and appreciated authors who acknowledged that God has designed human sexuality, in part at least, for married people's pleasure. Such authors described sexual pleasure as a priceless gift spouses can give to one another – a gift, in fact, that they *must* give to one another.

The notion of sex as something important we must give to our spouses is biblical. 1 Corinthians 7 teaches clearly that spouses must fulfil their 'marital duty' to one another, and must not 'deprive each other'. According to this passage, a wife does not have authority over her own body; her husband does. Similarly, she has authority over his. These verses are not-so-subtle reminders that we each owe our spouse a satisfying sexual relationship. We are, after all, our spouse's only sexual option. The commitment to marital fidelity, which every sincere Christian couple must make, means that if we don't find sexual fulfilment in our marriage, we don't find it. It is as simple, and sometimes as tragic, as that. Each of us must take our sexual responsibility seriously, and lovingly and enthusiastically do everything in our power to meet and fulfil our spouse's sexual needs and desires.

Having said all that, we want to briefly mention the flip side of healthy sex. We believe that putting too much emphasis on sex as something one does for his or her spouse can have a negative effect on some people's attitudes. For these people sex becomes one more obligation, one more task they need to perform to be a 'good wife' or a 'good husband'. They forget that sex is something they should enjoy *for themselves*.

Some people don't enjoy sex because they don't enjoy their own sexuality. Some husbands and wives, in fact, don't even view themselves as sexual beings. Sex is something they *do*, an out-of-character behaviour they squeeze in at the end of a busy day, rather than a natural extension of an important dimension of who they are. These people would become more interested and interesting sexual partners if they would give themselves permission to enjoy their sexuality, view their sexuality as an important part of their identity, and take delight in excelling sexually. People who take a positive approach to their sexuality, and commit themselves to developing their sexual skills just as they develop their other gifts and skills, cultivate a sexual confidence that frees them to become active rather than passive participants in a sexual relationship. They become proactive sexually rather than merely reactive. And they bring tremendous pleasure to their spouses.

L

Nappies. Dinner. Dishes. Sex. They were all part of the same routine, all part of my responsibility as a wife and mother. And all about equally enjoyable.

But somewhere along the way I began to see sex differently. I began to view it as a diversion, an escape, a chance to crawl out from under routine responsibilities and mundane chores. A chance to put on a new hat, to be somebody different. A chance to have some fun right in my own home, without having to buy a ticket or pay a baby-sitter. I began to view it as a break that I deserved, a romantic reward.

When I began to view sex as something fun I could do for myself, when I quit focusing my attention solely on what would make Bill happy and started thinking about what would please me as well, I became a much more exciting sexual partner. I no longer had to worry about pleasing Bill. I *was* pleasing him. He would say, in fact, that my new attitude marked a dramatically positive turning point in our sexual relationship. When a wife experiences maximum pleasure herself, that multiplies her husband's pleasure.

We're not talking about selfish sex. We assume that husbands and wives are committed to satisfying each other sexually, and that they will be sensitive to one another's unique needs and preferences and desires. What we're talking about is authentic, fully engaged, mutually enjoyable, genuinely fun sex.

Getting Started

Fun sex doesn't start in the bedroom. It starts in the kitchen, during a private moment when a nonsexual touch slides over into the realm of the blatantly sexual. It begins with a playful suggestion of sexual intent, or a not-so-subtle sexual innuendo, or a well-placed flirtatious remark.

B

Over the years we have developed our own *physical love language*. When I leave for the evening and Lynne whispers, 'If you make it home from your board meeting on time tonight, I'll make it worth your while,' I don't have to wonder what she means. I know that's an open invitation, and you can bet I get home on time. This may explain the efficiency of our board meetings!

When I'm travelling, and I call home and Lynne says, 'You don't know what you're missing tonight,' I know that's her way of telling me I have an interested wife waiting at home. And it seriously tempts me to hop a plane for O'Hare.

Another way to encourage sexual enthusiasm is to actively build one another's concept of desirability. Husbands and wives will be much more interested in sex if they feel like desirable sexual partners.

L

With the unavoidable media onslaught of strikingly beautiful, sexually stimulating, airbrushed female bodies, real live women need a heavy dose of sexual affirmation. We need to know that even though we don't have perfect bodies we have the power to excite and delight our husbands.

Bill constantly compliments me in specific, sexually oriented terms. He knows the physical characteristics I feel uncomfortable about, and sensitively reassures me about those. He also makes a big point of 'talking up' my positive physical attributes. He goes out of his way to convince me that my physical liabilities are of the sort that make little difference to him, while my assets are of the sort that make his day.

My sexual confidence, and my ability to enjoy my sexuality, are strongly tied to Bill's enthusiastic, consistent, verbal affirmation of my sexual desirability. Many spouses wish their husbands or wives had greater sexual interest and confidence. They don't realize the power they have to instil that confidence through affirmation and compliments.

How spouses dress is another way they can heighten – or squelch – sexual desire. We know that for some people dress truly makes little difference. Most spouses admit, however, that what their husband or wife wears affects their sexual interest.

$\boxed{L}$ One beautiful spring day Bill confiscated my favourite, well-worn nightgown, ripped it into irregular squares, and used it as a rag to wash the car. He had previously suggested that I terminate my love affair with that gown, but I hadn't taken him seriously. Now I had no choice.

I retaliated by spending an afternoon in the designer pyjama section of a department store looking for a replacement for Bill's favourite 'loungewear' – a torn T-shirt and baggy sweats.

Seriously, we have had some very frank discussions about dress. I have tended to be an overly modest, safe dresser. Bill has tended to be an overly casual, careless dresser. He finally admitted that he would prefer a little more pizzazz (a subtle seductive flair, he calls it) in my dress, particularly at home. I finally admitted that I would prefer a little more style in his dress, at home *and* abroad.

Maybe you think this is an insignificant point. After all, how we dress is a purely temporal concern, a relatively trivial issue in the scheme of life. But temporal or not, we have found that it affects the sexual climate in our marriage. So we think it's something worth paying attention to.

Maintaining good health is another way to enhance sexual interest. The general sense of well-being and increased body consciousness that come from regular exercise enhance sexuality. Eating right and getting enough sleep are important, too. Everybody knows that exhaustion is one of the greatest sex-busters.

Other sure sex-busters are hostility and lack of creativity, which is why we started this chapter the way we did. Working through hidden hostilities and learning to court creatively are essential to enhancing sexual interest.

Again – Talk, Talk, Talk

Each couple's physical relationship is unique. Some couples couldn't imagine a sexual encounter without music and candlelight. Others prefer silence and the cloak of darkness. For some people, exhaustion makes an evening rendezvous impractical; they prefer morning get-togethers. For others, even the thought of a morning sexual encounter is laughable. Preferred frequency of sex is also highly variable.

Instead of taking your cues from Hollywood or from other couples, why not develop your own sexual style. Experiment. Explore new avenues of sexual expression. And above all, communicate. Talk openly, vulnerably, specifically, and regularly about your sexual relationship. We have observed a direct correlation between a couple's level of sexual communication and their level of sexual fulfilment. Too many people expect their spouses to 'just know' what they want sexually, then do a slow burn when their spouses don't come through.

A more constructive option is to openly discuss issues directly related to sexuality. You might suggest ways your spouse could help you feel more desirable, and ask for ideas about how you could do the same in return. Another idea is to describe the kinds of circumstances, events, or conversations that are most likely to spark your sexual interest. You could also talk about guaranteed turnoffs, personal sex-busters, and past sexual disappointments. Or you could describe your best recent sexual memories, and explain what made those experiences so good. Sharing specific ideas about what you can each do, say, or wear to capture the other's sexual attention would also be helpful.

For some couples these questions are terribly threatening. Husbands and wives who have never talked openly about their sexual relationship often find it very hard to get started. Picking one question and discussing it after a day of lighthearted fun may be the best way for such couples to start. Eventually they can move into more in-depth discussions and even begin a little undercover research.

Sensitive, open communication is hefty challenge, whether you are discussing a backlog of anger or a way to spice up a less-than-sizzling sexual relationship. But it always pays high dividends. So give it a try. Prop up the pillows on your bed, make yourself comfortable, and talk openly with your spouse about sex. You just might be glad you did.

We were.

Living in Crisis Mode

B It was a Saturday morning in December of 1989. I went to my office early to finish the sermon I had to give that evening at church. At 5.30 a.m. I was on page twelve of my message. By 1.30 p.m. I was on page eight. I was in big trouble.

To complicate matters, I had to do a wedding before five hundred people that afternoon, and I hadn't given one thought to what I was going to say to the young people and their gathered family and friends. I thought about my unfinished message, about the wedding, and about the evening church service, and in a moment of total frustration, I laid my head down on my desk and cried.

Almost before the first teardrop hit the desk I reminded myself that falling apart was a ridiculous waste of time, and I quickly mopped myself up. But in that brief moment of 'losing it' I had seen the truth: the wheels were coming off my carefully constructed wagon.

That autumn our church had added another weekly service, which meant that I taught Wednesday, Thursday, and Saturday nights, and twice on Sunday morning. In between message preparation and actual teaching, I squeezed an increasing load of administrative duties and travel commitments. I had thought I was up to the challenge of an increased teaching schedule, and I had charged into the autumn months prepared to run the kingdom race as hard and fast as I'd ever run it before. But all of a sudden, it seemed I couldn't run at all.

I hobbled through autumn, hanging on till the Christmas holiday. I left with my family for what was supposed to be a quiet family retreat. Through unforeseen events, we ended up instead in a hotel mob scene. It was the kind of place where you had to wait twenty minutes for an elevator, and when the elevator came it was so crowded you couldn't get in. That was the last straw. I was in a mild state of frenzy the entire week.

When we got home I went alone to Wisconsin for three days to recuperate, think, and pray. 'God, what's happening to me? I don't understand what's going on in my life, but I feel like I'm going under. Help me.'

I spent the following year putting the pieces of my life back together. By delegating certain ministry responsibilities I was able to continue working, but at a greatly reduced pace. The remainder of my time I devoted to personal healing and to some long-overdue reflection on a pattern of life that had finally driven me to the breaking point.

Beware of Achilles' Heel

It was just a small spot of weakness on the mythical warrior's heel, but it led to his death in the Trojan War. Since classical times we have borrowed from the Greek legend the notion of a nagging vulnerability with the power to bring a strong man – or woman – down. Everyone has an Achilles' heel. The wise among us, who recognize their weaknesses and carefully protect them from attack, stand firm; the unwise, who leave their weaknesses exposed, are downed in the battle.

One problem with an Achilles' heel – whatever form it takes – is that it follows us into marriage. In this chapter and the next we want to expose our respective Achilles' heels because we have discovered, in looking back over seventeen years of marriage, that our individual weak spots have complicated our relationship more than anything else we have discussed thus far.

<u>L</u>   Bill's Achilles' heel is his overdevotion to work and ministry, and in the latter months of 1989 it almost ruined him.

It had nearly destroyed our relationship years before, but as we mentioned in a previous chapter, after five years of marriage Bill made some dramatic schedule changes. For the sake of our marriage and family life, he committed himself to maintaining our Thursday morning breakfast dates and to being home four nights a week. This commitment to being home more meant he regularly turned down requests to attend or speak at church meetings and at outside events. If his travel schedule interfered with time set aside for family, he made up the lost time as soon as possible: he scheduled a special outing with the kids or planned a make-up date with me. He also took an annual summer break, dedicated both to personal study and family fun. And he put time and creativity into planning family getaways throughout the year. He took our marriage and family life very, very seriously. Even when his work responsibilities increased he maintained his commitment to being home.

As the years passed, however, I began to see a change in Bill. More and more I sensed that he was home in body only. His mind was somewhere else, preoccupied with concerns that had nothing to do with home. Whereas in the past he had been an active contributor to our family life, he seemed now to have little to give. He wasn't unpleasant or unkind, but he was always exhausted. Home was where he came to crash. The kids and I had to tiptoe through the evening so as not to disturb him.

'Shh, Daddy's resting.'

'No, you can't disturb him now. He needs to recuperate.'

'Maybe you can talk to him tomorrow.'

He was home; he hadn't violated his commitment. But we certainly weren't enjoying his presence. He poured nearly all his energy into his work, and we got an empty, cracked shell we had to patch together and send back to the office.

Bill's Achilles' heel led him into a style of life so fast-paced it drained every ounce of emotional energy out of him and undermined our most earnest attempts to build a mutually satisfying marriage. He was living in what we call 'crisis mode'.

Keeping it Pegged in the Red

Crisis mode living is when you spend every waking moment of every day trying to figure out how to keep all your balls in the air and all your plates spinning. In crisis mode you keep running faster and faster, from project to project, deadline to deadline, quota to quota, meeting to meeting, sermon to sermon. Your RPMs keep creeping higher and higher until you hit the red line.

Most active people have to spend a certain amount of time in crisis mode. Life just turns out that way. You're an accountant during tax season. You repair air conditioners and it's August in Phoenix. You're cramming to take the bar exam. Your kids are breaking out with chicken pox. You have two weeks to meet a sales quota.

The problem arises when you spend too much time in crisis mode. That's when crisis mode goes from being a season of life to becoming a way of life. When that happens – when you keep the needle pegged in the red week after week, month after month – you start doing the only thing you can do. You economize. You shortchange your investment of energy in certain areas of your life so you can invest it in other areas – usually in the performance-oriented areas to which your self-esteem is tied. Nothing matters but keeping those all-important balls in the air and those ultimately significant plates spinning, so you use all your energy accomplishing those feats. In every other area of life, you become a miser; you hoard your energy, you engage minimally, you touch superficially, you slide along the surface, you *skim*.

First, you skim relationally. Your bond with your spouse that used to be strong and intimate becomes increasingly weak and distant. You hope he or she doesn't have a serious need because you don't have energy to deal with it. You hydroplane over conflicts. You put Band-Aids on serious problems. You resort to quick fixes, and pretend things really aren't so bad.

You also skim with your kids. You don't keep track of them too well any more. You no longer know what is going on in their lives. Little signs of trouble grab your attention, but you push them out of your mind. Warning flags wave, but you turn your head. You don't have the energy to face them – not now, anyway. Maybe tomorrow. Or maybe they will just go away.

Your friendships that used to be so deep and accountable are now characterized by shallowness. Your casual friendships don't even exist any more. Pretty soon, nobody has access to you because you are so busy juggling and spinning.

You also skim in your relationship with God. You reduce your prayers to cries of desperation. You reduce worship to thanking God for helping you survive the madness of another week. You run too fast for reflection or meditation, for introspection or confession. You begin rationalizing little sins, and then bigger ones. Before you know it, you have journeyed far from spiritual innocence.

Then you start skimming emotionally. You find that your anger is flaring up more than it used to, but you don't take time to figure out why. You no longer pay attention to feelings like hurt or sadness or guilt. You become a mechanical soldier: you just keep marching, doing what is necessary, and stuffing your feelings deeper and deeper inside. If you knew that those stuffed feelings were huddling together and planning an emotional insurrection that would one day scare the daylights out of you, you might pay attention to them. But you don't know that. Besides, you don't have the energy to go peeking under stones and trudging through the sticky muck of your emotional life. You don't have time to look inside.

Check *All* the Gauges

Even if you have time to consider your emotional condition, chances are you won't. The Christian community has a pretty good track record for ignoring the emotional side of life. When it comes to reading the gauges on the dashboard of their psyche, most Christians look at only one gauge: the spiritual one. They assume that if they are sincerely walking with Christ, if they are praying and receiving sound teaching, if they are worshipping publicly and privately, then everything is okay.

A few Christians go a step further and check out the physical gauge. They believe, as we do, that part of Christian obedience, part of making ourselves fully available for God's use, is to take care of their bodies. So they eat birdseed and tree bark, and lift weights and do aerobic exercises. They are convinced that if they keep the spiritual and physical gauges in order they will be able to work hard, stand firm, and win the battles until the day they die.

But as crucial as those gauges are, there is a third gauge, the emotional gauge, and neglecting to pay attention to it has been the downfall of many spiritually strong and physically healthy people.

We have observed that nearly everyone faces at least one massive, energy-draining reality. It may be a financial pressure or a health concern or a rebellious teenager. It could be a handicapped child or a personality conflict with a friend or neighbour. For some people it's a demanding boss or a pending lawsuit. Others get bogged down by the ongoing trauma of a difficult marriage, or the daily drain of a high-stress job. Sometimes it's just an unpleasant responsibility that can't be ignored. Whatever it is, it repeatedly drains one's emotional tanks.

In addition, people living in crisis mode usually face a long list of smaller energy-draining realities every day. So at the end of every 24-hour period, their emotional gauges read empty, and they end up living their lives in a constant state of emotional depletion.

A Shrinking Heart

The emotional depletion that results from living in crisis mode eventually produces a *shrinking heart*. This is a heart that does not worship as authentically as it once did, or love God as passionately as it used to. It is a heart that is no longer sensitive to the needs of others, a heart that has lost the fire of compassion.

While the hearts of healthy Christians keep enlarging to encompass more of the heart of Christ, the hearts of Christians in crisis mode become shrivelled and weak. A man from our church said, 'You're right about the crisis mode. I have a bigger staff, a bigger budget, a bigger building, a bigger house, a bigger bank account, and a bigger belt line than I had five years ago. And all I have to show for it is a hollow cavern where my heart used to be.'

B   I know exactly what that man meant. I learned about it firsthand during the summer following the emotional crash described at the beginning of this chapter. Though I had begun to make some necessary life changes, I was still depleted emotionally when Lynne and the kids and I arrived in Michigan for our annual summer break.

The day after we arrived I talked with a friend in a local store. Just as we ended our conversation and I headed for the exit door, I noticed a Vietnam veteran in a motorized wheelchair whom I had seen around town the previous summer. He was leaving the store too, and arrived at the exit shortly ahead of me. While I waited impatiently for him to jockey his wheelchair through the narrow doorway, an unsettling awareness began churning inside me.

I sensed the Holy Spirit saying, 'Take a look inside you right now, Bill. Isn't it true that you are more upset about the inconvenience of waiting thirty seconds to get out this door than about the broken dreams this man carries in his motorized wheelchair? Isn't it true that your trivial inconvenience causes you more heartache than this man's tragedy?'

I walked to my car thinking, *What's wrong with me? I used to love people. I used to have compassion. I used to be moved by the lost, the needy, the hurting. Now all I care about is my convenience: 'Don't bother me, pal. Get out of my way.' I ought to be arrested!*

I spent the next four or five weeks replenishing myself emotionally. I separated myself from the pressures of ministry. I read for pleasure. I did fun, relaxing activities with my family. I enjoyed lighthearted conversations with close friends. I spent time alone.

One afternoon I was out running, and I saw that same Vietnam vet coming down the other side of the street in his wheelchair. When he was directly across the street from me I turned to look at him. Our eyes met, and it was like God gave me X-ray vision. I felt as if I were peering deep into his soul, and I began to cry over the heartbreak of his life. He was just about my age, and had probably dreamed the same dreams and held the same aspirations that I had dreamed and held in my youth. But somewhere in a hostile jungle he had stepped on a land mine, and his whole life had come crashing in on him.

He turned and wheeled up a concrete ramp into a tiny clapboard cottage, and I was saddened to see him disappear. I wanted to reach out to him, talk to him, show him that I cared. I was filled with a swell of emotion.

While I continued my run, I thought about what had happened. I sensed the Holy Spirit saying, 'You're on your way back, Bill. Your emotional tanks are filling, and you're starting to feel again. You're beginning to have compassion again.'

Seduced by Sin

While emotional depletion is often ignored, the havoc it plays in our lives cannot be ignored. In addition to draining the compassion out of our hearts, emotional depletion also leaves us vulnerable to sin. People who are emotionally exhausted, or whose emotions have been neglected, begin to cry out on a psychological level for comfort, for release, for escape, for something that will make them feel good or satiate their senses. They begin to crave quick hits of pleasure. They are lured by temptations that had never tempted them before. Activities they had never considered suddenly become live options.

$\boxed{B}$ I couldn't figure out what was going on in me during the months before my summer break. I kept recalling a song recorded by Burt Reynolds: 'Let's Do Something Cheap and Superficial'. The tantalizing words kept playing over and over in my mind.

I didn't fall to that which tempted me, but I talked to others who had. I told them about my emotional depletion, and about my nagging desire to escape in ways I had never considered before. Over and over I heard the same response.

'That's how I felt before I fell to sin.'

'That's what led to my demise.'

'That's where I went wrong.'

In the previous chapter we mentioned that a Christian man who had committed adultery challenged us to make fun a priority in our marriage. He also told us to keep careful watch over our emotional gauges. 'Don't let the tanks run low,' he warned. 'When you get emotionally drained, you begin to crave a quick fix. And too often quick fixes present themselves in the form of illicit relationships. There's something about a clandestine meeting or a secret conversation that provides the kind of fast-acting high an emotionally depleted person craves. But it's a high that guarantees a bad trip.'

Opt for a Slow Charge

If a fast-acting high isn't the answer to emotional depletion, what is? A trickle charge.

If you were to go out in your garage and turn on every accessory in your car, you could probably drain the battery in about five minutes. To recharge it, you would have two choices. First, there is the quick charge. This is a fast-acting method that gets cars running in record time, but if used frequently it burns out the plates in the battery. Second, there is the method all responsible mechanics suggest: the trickle charge. With this approach, it takes six to eight hours to get a battery recharged to full strength, but it doesn't burn out the plates. It replaces the lost energy *and* preserves the life of the battery.

Drained emotional batteries need a trickle charge, too. A trickle charge involves determining what replenishes you emotionally and then incorporating that into your schedule. It also means spacing your emotionally draining responsibilities in such a way that in between them you can trickle charge back up to emotional fullness. In our culture that is no small challenge.

Today's modern technology makes it possible for men and women to carry tremendous amounts of responsibility and to make every minute count. A pastor can conduct planning meetings on his car phone on the way to the airport, write sermons on his lap-top computer on the plane, speak in five cities in two days, and fax up-to-the-minute memos to his church staff. And that story is repeated in every other profession.

We finish one emotionally draining activity and have fifteen minutes before the next one starts. We run to the microwave, slide in a plate of pasta, and after thirty seconds, complain that 'this thing takes forever!' The speed of our lives makes it impossible to recharge.

In Jesus' day, it may well have been easier to live a balanced life. Imagine that after speaking to a crowd in Jerusalem, Jesus decides to walk the fifteen or so miles to Jericho with his twelve disciples. They walk for a couple of hours, then stop to cool off under a fig tree. They tell a few jokes, eat a few grapes, then slowly move on. A while later they pause at a well and chat with other travellers watering their camels, then they enjoy a drink themselves before hitting the road again. Before they know it, it's dinner time, so they wander off the beaten path to gather wood for a fire. They quickly build a flaming pyramid of dry branches, but it takes some time for the coals to get hot. By the time dinner is done, it's dusk – no time to travel – so they settle in for the night, gathering round the roaring blaze to talk over the day.

We don't mean to minimize the rigours of first-century travel, but it's more than likely that something very healthy happened during those long hours of mundane activity. There was physical exercise, friendly conversation, long stretches of quiet for reflection and planning, and plenty of time for emotional reserves to trickle charge before the next draining demand.

B

That healthy pattern was definitely not a part of my life. Crisis mode living never leaves time for a trickle charge. So my first step in building up my emotional reserves was to get out of crisis mode.

I realized that what had shoved me into crisis mode was too much teaching. I was spending almost every waking moment of every day thinking about, praying about, reading about, writing about, preparing for, or recuperating from giving messages. Even when I was meeting with my staff, or spending an evening with friends, or relating to Lynne and the kids, I was feeling the weight of message preparation, and I was preoccupied.

I prayed about the situation, and sensed that the answer was a team approach to teaching at our church, but most Christian leaders from whom I sought counsel said it wouldn't work. *You can't have more than one primary teacher in a given church. The congregation will be torn. It will split the church. There will be competition between teachers. Lines of authority will blur. The staff management structure will crumble. It is too radical. Too risky.*

But I knew that I needed to make a radical change. The size of my heart depended on it. The shape of my marriage depended on it. I had to take the risk.

In the autumn of 1990 I divvied up a year's worth of weekend and midweek services between myself and three other teachers. Contrary to some people's fear, the change has been overwhelmingly positive for our church. And for me, it has proven to be exactly what I needed. I have been able to escape the madness of crisis mode living and enter a whole new way of life.

Playing Games

But getting out of crisis mode is only the beginning. Reorganizing our lives and establishing a more manageable schedule opens time for a trickle charge. But then we need to discover the specific activities that can provide the charge and replenish us emotionally. We need to incorporate into our schedules the forms of recreation that truly do 'recreate' us.

B It didn't take me long to figure out what I had to do. In fact, when I looked back over the years I could see clearly why I had ended up emotionally exhausted. When I first went into ministry I had all kinds of hobbies and recreational thrills and chills. Athletics were a big part of my life – I loved car and motorcycle racing, snow skiing, flying, water skiing, football, softball, basketball – and they were effective energizers and stress reducers. My ministry demands were also much lighter then, so I had relatively low responsibility and a lot of fun and recreation.

Between 1973 and 1989, however, my responsibilities skyrocketed, while my rest and recreational levels plummeted: I no longer had time for playing games. So at thirty-eight years old, I ended up with a heavy mantle of ministry pressure draped across my shoulders, and almost no recreational releases.

After my crash, I realized I had to slow down enough to reintegrate recreational athletics into my life. During the summer of 1990 I enrolled in a professional race driving school to address my 'need for speed'. I also experienced the adrenaline rush of learning how to barefoot ski – and taught Lynne how, too. In the autumn I joined a Park District football league, and I even played a little golf. It was like hooking myself up to an IV dripping undiluted emotional energy. Every week I felt healthier than I had the week before.

Along the way, I found my shrunken heart beginning to stretch; I felt levels of compassion I hadn't felt in years. And I thought of the sins that had previously tempted me with disbelief. *You mean I was allured by* that? *I must have been out of my mind!*

The sad thing about emotional depletion is that it makes sincere, godly people act as if they are 'out of their minds'. It twists personalities and alters behaviour to the point where people become nearly unrecognizable to co-workers, friends, and spouses. Ultimately, it drives people to hurt those they love the most.

In contemporary Western culture we tend to view recreation as a luxury, as something to engage in if we have nothing important or productive to do. This isn't true for everyone, of course. Surely, some people reading these pages could justifiably accuse their spouses of being too devoted to recreation, or too 'slowed down'. Many people, however, would serve themselves, their spouses, and their families well by playing a few more games, learning to relax, by discovering recreational outlets that refresh them. Far from being a luxury, it may be a necessary antidote to chronic emotional fatigue.

Let's Get Together Again

Another way to fill emotional tanks is by enjoying replenishing relationships.

Like us, you have probably been involved in three types of relationships. First, there are draining relationships, the kind that sap your energy. The people may be nice, but for some reason you don't click; or they always seem to want something from you and never offer anything back. During an hour spent with such a couple you check your watch six times, and after they leave you suggest to your spouse that you schedule your next get-together in the year 2025. It's not that you dislike them, but you always feel empty when they leave.

Next, there are neutral relationships. They don't drain you exactly; the people take a little, but they also give a little back in return, so it ends up being a wash. Still, such relationships don't really enhance your life and you're not highly motivated to maintain them.

Finally, there are replenishing relationships, which breathe life into you. You visit another couple, and after what seems like minutes you say, 'I can't believe it's 11:30. Where did the evening go?' On the way home you wonder aloud to your spouse what your friends are doing next Friday night. You have no hidden agenda. You don't need anything from them, nor do you feel an obligatory responsibility toward them; you don't have to counsel or 'fix' them. You just like being with them. You can prop your feet up on the coffee table and relax. You can talk freely. There's a natural ebb and flow in your relationship, and when you part ways everyone feels refreshed, energized, and lighthearted.

We have found that many people, particularly those in the helping professions, have some neutral relationships, many draining ones, and few, if any, replenishing friendships. Is it any woder they feel emotionally depleted? Jesus seemed to be far more balanced in His relational world. He intentionally exposed himself to draining people – the masses who tugged at Him, sought healing, and asked an endless stream of questions. And He appeared to have some fairly neutral relationships with friends and disciples who followed Him but remained on the fringes of His life. But there also seemed to be a number of replenishing people in Jesus' life. He often slipped away with Peter, James, and John and frequently stopped by the home of Mary, Martha, and Lazarus. He needed time with people who replenished His spirit, and built Him up, and gave Him the freedom to relax. We think one reason Jesus broke down at Lazarus' tomb was that He had lost a replenishing brother.

Part of being a Christian is to give to those who can give nothing in return. If we claim to follow Jesus, we should intentionally pursue some draining relationships, as He did, and some neutral ones as well. But we must not overload our relational world with draining and neutral people. If Jesus needed replenishing relationships, how much more do we?

It's Worth It!

[B] Ending up in a teary pile on my desk on a busy Saturday afternoon was one of the best things that ever happened to me. Desperation made me face up to what crisis mode living and emotional depletion had done to me and to my relationship with the people I love, and it motivated me to do something about it.

It forced me to take one of the greatest ministry risks I have ever taken. It gave me the freedom to incorporate recreation into my life without feeling guilty about doing something so 'unproductive'. And it motivated me to get my relational life in better balance. It was obvious why I had little to offer Lynne and the kids: I was giving so much of my relational energy to draining people. I have since focused more attention on replenishing relationships, and they have recharged me and enhanced by marriage and family life.

It wasn't easy to make these changes, and there may be people who don't agree with the steps I've taken. But I can wholeheartedly say that getting out of crisis mode living was worth the price I had to pay. It is great to be relating to staff members as people again. To have friends who hold me accountable again. To have time to be actively involved with my kids again. To have creative energy to pour into my marriage again.

I'd like to shout it from the mountaintops: *It is worth whatever radical change it takes to get out of crisis mode. It is worth it!*

Dare to Downshift

Can you relate to this Achilles' heel? Are your emotional batteries low? Has your heart shrunk? Has the love drained out of your relationships? Do you think you might be heading for a crash?

If you are living in crisis mode, Beware. It *will* catch up with you, and it *will* undermine your marriage and family life. So please, don't rush from one emotionally draining activity to the next. Don't live so fast that you never have time for replenishing recreation or relationships. Don't neglect your need to trickle charge.

Perhaps you, too, need to make some radical changes in your life. Maybe you need to revise your job description. Or cut down on travel commitments. Maybe you need to resign from that board or drop that extra class. Another answer may be to refuse to take on so many projects, or hire some extra help, or downscale your goals. You may even have to take a demotion or say no to a wonderful opportunity – or a whole fistful of opportunities. How good, after all, is an opportunity that throws you into crisis mode? How great is a lifestyle that never gives you time to enjoy life?

In her cutting-edge book, *Downshifting*, Amy Saltzman, an associate editor for *U.S. News & World Report*, describes the 'gracious romantic porches' that adorn the homes on Newark Street in Washington, DC. She calles them 'tailor-made for reading Faulkner, chatting with the neighbors, watching the world go by'.[1] Yet she admits that during all her walks down Newark Street she had never seen anyone actually sitting on those enviably perfect porches. Successful young professionals dashed up and down the steps, but none had time to stop. That, Saltzman claims, 'said it all' about the unhealthy pace of too many people's lives.

Saltzman suggests creative, practical ways for emotionally drained fast-trackers to 'downshift' into more enjoyable patterns of life. People, she says, must redefine success in their own terms, and live according to those new images.

> The new pictures in [downshifters'] heads are more eloquent, thoughtful and, ultimately, more satisfying. The front porch may not be as grand or the house it is attached to as large. But in this new picture, they are sitting on that porch, chatting with the neighbors, writing a letter to a friend and rereading that favourite old classic.[2]

People living in crisis mode rarely sit on front porches and chat with neighbours. They rarely write letters to friends or reread favourite books. And, may we add, they rarely have warm, satisfying marriages.

But we, like the downshifters in Saltzman's book, are living proof that such patterns can change.

What About You?

Of course, you may not be living in crisis mode. Maybe the threat of emotional depletion isn't your Achilles' heel. But, unless you are a remarkable exception to the rule, you do have a weak spot. You do have an area of vulnerability.

Perhaps you have an uncontrollable temper fed by unresolved issues from your past, or childhood memories that haunt you and make you withdraw from your spouse. Maybe you have low self-esteem that causes you to become unreasonably jealous or insecure. Perhaps you don't relate well to your parents and you take out your frustration on your spouse.

If this chapter does nothing else, we hope it will motivate you to discover your Achilles' heel, acknowledge the negative effect it has on you as an individual and as a marriage partner, and take steps to become healthy, whole, and strong.

B

We're not suggesting it will be easy or that changes can be made quickly. It took a solid year for me to make my journey back to wholeness. But at the end of that year, I felt like a different person. I had energy for life again. I was a contributor to my family again. I was excited about my marriage again.

And none too soon. Little did I know what was taking shape in the heart and mind of my long-suffering wife.

Notes

1. Amy Saltzman, *Downshifting* (New York: HarperCollins *Publishers*, 1991), p.13.
2. Saltzman, *Downshifting*, p. 224.

Getting Lost Along the Way

L 'I love you, I just can't seem to handle being married to you. After sixteen years of marriage, I don't know who I am anymore. My life seems to have gotten lost in yours.'

It was Thanksgiving evening. With the fragrance of a well-stuffed turkey still filling the house, the words tumbled out. But the issues that prompted them had begun to surface the previous May. In the early morning hours of what had been a sleepless spring night, I had poured out my heart to my computer.

'I can't go on like this,' I wrote. 'I can't live this life anymore. I keep rushing, rushing, rushing, rushing. I keep going, moving, doing, covering all the bases, responding to all the demands, the wishes, the suggestions, the oughts. I wish I could sleep for a week. I wish I could run away. But there are too many responsibilities. Bill is counting on me. I need to come through, like I always do.

'But I am so tired. I feel so empty. It's like someone drained the life out of me.

'I feel like a robot ... but not quite. I wish I were a robot. Then I could just program myself to do everything I am supposed to do. And not care. And not desire. And not feel. And not hurt. And not have a little core of individuality that yelps occasionally.

'Is this what life is supposed to be? Is this the best I can do?'

Throughout the summer months the frustration, the emptiness, intensified. I felt increasingly like a vacuous shell, like an image with no substance. I realized, as I looked deep inside, that there was 'nobody home'. There was no person inside. No *me*.

I looked back through the years to a time when I had 'existed'. I saw a rosy newborn cradled in her father's arms. I saw a toddler spilling sand into buckets on a white beach. I saw a first-grader in a ribboned Easter bonnet standing lady-like by her mother's side. I saw a ten-year-old riding a pony across the green pasture behind an old farmhouse. I saw a teenager cheering for the Mustangs at a high school football game. I saw love and acceptance and fun and enthusiasm and happiness. I saw a childhood rich in the riches worth having.

So why, as an adult, did I feel so empty? So exhausted? So poor? So much like a … like a victim?

That was it! That was the word I had been looking for for months. I felt like a victim. A victim of life. A victim of Bill's life. His life had overpowered mine, swallowed up mine, erased mine.

Caught in the Air Pocket

Many people feel like victims of other people's behaviours and choices. Family members of alcoholics feel like victims of their loved one's drinking. Wives who are battered feel like victims of their spouse's uncontrollable temper. Some people feel like victims of another person's financial irre-sponsibility, or drug abuse, or unhealthy sexual desires. People with addictions or other compulsive disorders often litter the trail of their lives with friends and family members who feel like victims, who feel like their lives have been destroyed by another person's problem.

L

I didn't go so far as to say that my life had been destroyed. But I certainly felt that it had been sucked dry by Bill's overdevotion to work and ministry. We called it his Achilles' heel, but giving it a clever name didn't make it any less frustrating to me. I was tired of having to live with it.

Bill's work demanded nearly all his time and energy for many years. That meant I had to handle virtually every home/family/parenting responsibility. Did something break? Was someone sick? Did the bills have to be paid? Did the kids need a ride? Did something need to be cleaned, or bought, or cooked, or washed, or mowed, or maintained? Then I had to do it – or find someone to help me.

Even at the five-year point in our marriage, when Bill made a serious commitment to being home, that didn't change. He became more involved relationally with the kids and me, for which I was grateful. In fact, in many ways he became a model father; the kids did – and still do – adore him, feel very loved by him, and know they are a top priority to him: But he still had no time to devote to the practical, time-consuming, daily tasks of maintaining a home and family life.

In addition, there were the church responsibilities that 'drew me in' simply because I was the minister's wife. There were people to relate to and events to attend and notes to answer and calls to return and parties to host.

Then there was Bill's speaking/travelling ministry. Though he tried to keep his travel schedule to a minimum, the opportunities became increasingly difficult to turn down. Often I joined him, either because it was a couples' event and my presence was expected, or because I feared the detachment caused by frequent separations. The net result was that I travelled far more than I wanted to, and spent innumerable hours making childcare arrangements, writing instructions, and repacking suitcases that became tattered from overuse.

I seemed to be constantly moving, working, striving. It wasn't that what I was doing was so awful. Some women would have been delighted to live my life. But it wasn't right for me. I was an introvert living an extroverted life. A slow-paced person in a constant rush. A homebody hopping planes. I lived with a constant stomach ache – nervous butterflies that refused to be still. And I seldom got a good night's sleep. I often went to bed dreading the next day, and awoke disappointed that it had arrived so soon.

The biggest problem was that I seldom had time to do the things I wanted to do. I knew I had gifts and abilities, and at times throughout the years I tried to develop and use them. But that added so much rush and chaos to life that it was hardly worth it. Bill's work and gifts and pursuits so consumed me that I didn't have time for a life of my own. I felt more like an appendage to his life than a person in my own right.

Bill wasn't insensitive to the situation. Frequently during recent years he had urged me to make changes, to state my needs, to live how I wanted to live. But I didn't know how or where to start. I didn't know how to break the pattern. Bill raced through life, and repeatedly I got caught in the air pocket that trailed him.

I seemed to have no option, so I tried to accept it. But on an early morning in May I realized I couldn't accept it, and by midsummer I had begun to view myself as a victim. In the autumn I felt something churning deep inside – something ugly and unwanted, something I couldn't control. I was angry with an anger that had been building for years.

I thought I had dealt with my anger. I thought the pain addressed in carefully constructed peace talks was all the pain there was. I thought the poisonous ooze that had broken through the surface occasionally was the extent of my hostility. Now I realized there was something deeper, buried beneath years of disappointment and frustration.

But suddenly it was refusing to stay buried. Suddenly it was exploding. And sobbing. And pounding. And shouting.

It was Thanksgiving day, and I was not thankful. I was bitter and resentful. I was tired of having to worry about *Bill's* needs, *Bill's* desires, *Bill's* convenience, *Bill's* plans. I was tired of helping him live his life and having no time or energy to live my own.

Giving Till it Hurts

Those words grieve us. They are written in the past tense, but just barely. The pain they reveal is still fresh. The wounds have not yet healed. In fact, the ending to the story is only now being written.

We began working on this chapter on a blustering, Midwest morning in March. The previous weeks had been a flurry of ministry demands, out-of-state trips, and writing deadlines. It had been the kind of jumbled schedule that magnifies our temperament differences, highlights our communication weaknesses, and stretches our conflict resolution skills to the breaking point. We wore painted smiles to social functions, fulfilled our work responsibilities joylessly, and both fought the trapped feeling described in the early pages of this book. Romance had temporarily become a thing of the past.

When we finally had time to talk, it wasn't fun. We started facing one another at the kitchen table. We moved our discussion to the couch in the family room. We ended up seated on the bedroom floor, slumped against opposite walls.

We walked about our marriage and about the past. We talked about Thanksgiving and about anger. We talked about crisis mode and victims. The conversation was painful, shooting off on emotionally charged tangents and racing through two decades of relational mine fields. But it was also constructive. Peering through the tears, we discovered answers. We began to make sense out of the journey we'd been on together.

B We began to see how Lynne had fallen headlong into an unhealthy caretaker role. She had gotten so involved trying to take care of me, trying to rescue and protect me from the perils of crisis mode living, that she had neglected to take care of herself. She had ignored, or submerged, her needs, desires, feelings, and preferences. Finally, the neglect had caught up with her. She felt empty inside, she felt used and unappreciated, and understandably, she felt resentful.

Caretaking is a normal and healthy part of life. Parents are caretakers for their young children. Adult children often become caretakers for their elderly parents. Doctors and nurses are caretakers for the sick. Caretaking is healthy when we take care of those who legitimately need someone to take care of them – an infant or a sick friend, for example – and when we sincerely want to offer our help.

When we violate those guidelines, however, caretaking becomes unhealthy. When we do something we don't really want to do, when we say yes when we mean no, when we do things for people who are capable of and should be doing them for themselves, when we do more than our fair share when our help is requested, and when we fail to ask for what we want, need, and desire, we are involved in unhealthy caretaking, or rescuing.[1]

People rescue other people for a variety of reasons. Some people have low self-esteem and only feel worthy when they are helping others. They need to be needed. They believe the only way to earn love is to serve ceaselessly.

Some people have been taught that if they refuse to help someone else they are selfish. They think it is wrong to disappoint someone or hurt their feelings by saying no. They have believed the lie that it is self-centred to think about themselves, and impolite to mention personal wants and needs.[2]

Women sometimes believe that constant caretaking is their duty. Good wives and mothers, they think, should devote themselves to caretaking no matter how old their children are or how capable their husbands are, and no matter how little time they have to care for themselves.

Others rescue because they believe it is a charitable deed, even a godly one. 'Love your neighbour as yourself,' the Bible says. 'Go the extra mile.' 'Put on a heart of compassion.' So they do. But they forget to love themselves in the process. They end up crawling the extra mile on weary hands and knees. They think it is cruel and cold-blooded to let people work through legitimate feelings, or suffer consequences of irresponsible behaviour. So they let compassion turn to unhealthy caretaking.[3]

Acts of kindness and service are desirable. Giving what we want to give to those we love and to those who truly need our help is a privilege and a pleasure. Such acts make our homes, churches, and communities warm, inviting, life-giving places. But we need to establish limits in giving. 'Giving to and doing things for and with people are essential parts of healthy living and healthy relationships,' says counsellor and author Melody Beattie. 'But learning when not to give, when not to give in, and when not to do things for and with people are also essential parts of healthy living and healthy relationships.'[4]

She adds that excessive caretakers 'have misinterpreted the suggestions to "give until it hurts". We continue giving long after it hurts, usually until we are doubled over in pain. It's good to give some away, but we don't have to give it all away. It's okay to keep some for ourselves.'[5]

Our Lives Clashed...

L   It wasn't hard to understand how I had slipped into excessive caregiving. I am by temperament compassionate and empathetic, so it was easy for me to push the biblical teaching on giving and loving to the outer limit. Also, I recognized that when I helped Bill carry his load I was ultimately helping the church and facilitating Bill's expanding ministry around the world. I think I could have stood up to the marketplace. If Bill had been in business I think I would have said, 'For the sake of money, or position, or your ego, I won't do this.' But it was for the advancement of God's kingdom. How could I say no to that?

My nearly ideal upbringing also made it hard for me to say no. I enjoyed a charmed childhood and a remarkably warm and peaceful home environment. There was an easy temperament blend between my parents and me and, therefore, little conflict. My parents encouraged me and cheered me on without pushing me, so I never felt an undue pressure to win their approval. I was responsible and never went through a rebellious era, so they were free to give me few rules, a flexible curfew, and an unusual measure of freedom. Compared to most parent/adolescent relationships, ours was a dream.

The only problem was that I never developed a fighting spirit. I never learned to confront people or to stand up for myself. I never learned to set limits, to say, 'This is me. This is as far as I go. You can't push me any further.' My home life was so safe, so easy, so comfortable, such a natural fit that I never had to learn those skills.

Then I married Bill, and the strength and independence and self-assurance that had initially drawn me to him began to overpower me. I loved him, but I didn't know how to stand up against his strength. I didn't know how to break through his independence. My self-assurance shrivelled in the shadow of his.

Our temperaments clashed and I didn't know how to hang on to mine. Our preferences clashed and I didn't know how to assert mine. Our needs clashed and I didn't know how to get mine met.

Our lives clashed and I lost.

This Is Me!

One reason some people lose such battles is that they have failed to establish what psychologists call *boundaries*.

Dr Henry Cloud says, 'Boundaries are a property line. They define who we are and who we are not... Boundaries give us a sense of limits as to what is part of us and what is not part of us, what we will allow and what we won't allow.'[6]

Boundaries help us determine where we end and others begin, and what is our responsibility and what is someone else's. They help us determine how we will relate to others and protect us from being overpowered by others. Boundaries enable us to build close, vulnerable relationships with family members and friends without losing that very critical sense of separateness that defines who we are as individuals. People who fail to establish strong and healthy boundaries often end up feeling the kind of anguish described in the early pages of this chapter.

The most obvious aspect of personhood that lies within our boundaries is physical: our physical body clearly defines us and separates us from others. Other aspects of our personhood may be less obvious, but are no less critical to our definition of who we are. These are our attitudes, our feelings, our behaviours, our thoughts, our abilities, our wants, our choices, our limits, and our negative assertions.

People with strong boundaries take responsibility for these aspects of their personhood. They admit their feelings – whether they are sad or mad or glad or scared – and deal with them. They discover their abilities and take active steps to develop them. They acknowledge their wants, express them, and, if appropriate, satisfy them. They make choices for themselves so that they don't become controlled by other people's choices. They know their limits and live within them, so they don't get overextended. They confidently make negative assertions: No, that isn't me. No, I don't want to do that. No, I don't like that. They know who they are, and they aren't afraid to let other people know who they are.

People with weak boundaries aren't quite so sure who they are. They are not in touch with their separateness from others. They don't understand where their responsibility for others ends and their responsibility for themselves begins. They often end up being more affected by what others feel, think, want, or choose, than what they feel, think, want, or choose themselves.

A Setup

Learning about boundaries helped us understand some of the difficult dynamics in our marriage.

B   Growing up in my family, I had to develop a strong sense of boundaries. My dad had a very powerful personality. He was dominant, secure, confident, and intimidating to many people. His approval meant the world to me, but I realized at a young age that I could not afford to let his disapproval shape my choices. In order to survive under his authority, I had to risk standing up to him.

Though I never heard a definition of psychological boundaries when I was growing up, I definitely developed them. When I was nineteen years old, I put them to the ultimate test.

Early on a spring morning, I walked into his corner office and said, 'Dad, this is a great company and I know you would like me to help run it. But God is calling me in a different direction. I think He wants me to go into Christian work. I'm leaving the business.'

I walked out of his office shaking under the weight of his obvious displeasure and disappointment. I prayed, 'God, what do I do? The person I respect and love more than anyone else on this planet has just said no to what You want me to say yes to. What am I going to do?'

I thought about twelve-year-old Jesus, standing in the synagogue in Jerusalem, informing Mary and Joseph that He had to pursue His '[Heavenly] Father's business'.

I thought about the adult Jesus, startling His followers with these words: 'If anyone comes to me and does not hate [love me more than] his father and mother, his wife and children, his brothers and sisters – yes, even his own life – he cannot be my disciple' (Luke 14:26).

There is a time, the Bible seemed to be telling me, when you have to make up your own mind about things. You have to make your own choices about what to believe and who to follow. Someday you will stand accountable before a holy God, and you won't be able to hide in the shadow of your parents. So, step up to the plate and assume responsibility for your life. You're a big person. Make your own choice.

Several days later I went back into my dad's office and said, 'Dad, you can cut me out of everything, if you have to – even a relationship with you. But I have to do what God is calling me to do. I would love to have your approval, and if you can't give it to me, I'm going to walk around with a gaping hole in my heart. But I am going to do what God is calling me to do.'

That boundary battle marked my life. Though my dad died before he could see much of the fruit of my ministry, he did eventually support my decision. But even if he hadn't, I would have stood firm in my choice. I had learned to make tough decisions, to hold on to my opinions, and to fight for what I believed was right.

I acquired that ability in my youth, practised it in young adulthood, and carried it with me into my ministry and into my marriage.

As Lynne said, she walked into marriage without having learned to stand up for herself, to claim her rights, to draw her boundaries. I, on the other hand, walked into marriage with my boundaries very clearly staked out. Is it any wonder Lynne's life got swallowed up in mine?

Crossed Boundaries

Excessive caretakers, or people with weak boundaries, often look extremely responsible – and they are – for other people. But they don't take responsibility for themselves. They tend to worry more about how others feel than how they feel, solve other people's problems instead of their own, yield to other people's desires and deny their own, and live with the consequences of other people's choices and fail to choose for themselves. They frequently take what others think more seriously than what they think, and often facilitate the development of other people's skills and abilities and neglect the development of their own. In short, they assume the responsibility for other people's success, welfare, and happiness, and fail to assume that same responsibility for themselves.

As we said earlier, they often believe that such behaviour is right and necessary, perhaps even their Christian duty. But regardless of their motivation, they end up in the same unhappy condition: frustrated, angry and resentful.

Excessive caretaking appears to be a loving thing to do. But it isn't. It actually produces what Melody Beattie calls a 'triangle of hate'. People rescue others in unhealthy ways. Later they get mad at those they have rescued because they felt forced to do things they didn't want to do. Then they feel used and sorry for themselves. This pattern fosters self-hate, and generates negative feelings towards other people.[7]

B For years I accused Lynne of not being supportive of me. It wasn't that she failed to help me in practical ways; on the contrary, she was constantly offering me her tangible support. But there was something unpleasant in her attitude towards me. She claimed to love me, but I often felt her disapproval, her dislike. It seemed as if she were angry with me much of the time.

Now I realize she was. She tried hard not to be, because she truly believed she was pleasing God by serving me. But she went too far and gave up too much of herself – her needs, her desires, her wants, her preferences. She had allowed me to cross her boundaries, and the anger was inevitable. Even though she tried to pray it away, it lingered. Even though she tried to bury it, it leached through her layers of good intentions and tainted our relationship. Eventually, it exploded.

Taking Care of *Me*

Many relationships are laced with the anger of crossed boundaries. Many people resent the fact that their parent or child or spouse always gets his or her way. They resent feeling that they have to rescue people. They resent never having the time or freedom to live their own life. But that can change. There is a way to move out of resentment.

It is called personal empowerment. It means that people start taking care of themselves. They reclaim the responsibility for their lives, for their happiness, and for their future. They own their plight. They quit focusing on what someone else has done to them and start thinking about what they need to do for themselves. They start behaving as adults and making choices they can live with. They give themselves permission to feel their feelings. They start doing what they want to do. They admit their needs and, when appropriate, ask other people to help meet their needs. They quit calling themselves victims – and quit acting like victims.

Many of these victims really were true victims at some point in their lives: victims of abuse, neglect, abandonment, alcoholism, or some other situation against which they truly were helpless to protect themselves. But many people perpetuate their victimization, or even create it, by *allowing* other people to take advantage of them. Part of their healing process is to acknowledge their part in their victimization.[8] If they helped get themselves into the situation they are in, it follows that they have the power to get themselves out.

Dr Cloud says,

As an adult, you have choices. Take responsibility for them and own them. If you are giving something, you at some level are making a choice to do it; stop acting as if others make you give to them. If you are working somewhere that you do not like, take responsibility for finding something else. If you are criticized by a friend, take responsibility for the fact that you agree to meet with him or her. You are responsible for what you choose to do. *You can change your life by refusing to play victim* [italics ours].[9]

Another part of the healing process is for victims to forgive those who have truly caused hurt or offence, or who have taken advantage of them. Most people who feel victimized have tried forgiveness – time and time again. But each time the anger and resentment return, they realize that their attempt to forgive didn't work. Obviously, they assume, they weren't sincere or caring or godly enough; so on top of their other troubles they heap loads of guilt. Often, however, the real reason their forgiveness doesn't 'work' is that they are still allowing the other person to hurt them, or take advantage of them, or overpower them. Only when they begin taking responsibility for their lives, and crawl out from under the burden of another person's problem, can they really forgive. Melody Beattie says, 'Forgiveness comes in time – in its own time – if we are striving to take care of ourselves ... If we are taking care of us, we will understand what to forgive and when it's time to do that."[10]

When we start acting like adults and taking responsibility for our lives, we force other people to act like adults too, and to face the consequences of their actions. This is better for us, and it ends up being better for them too.

L

I realize now that one reason Bill lived in crisis mode for so long was that I 'enabled' him to. By pouring my time and energy into picking up the pieces of his whirlwind life, I made it possible for him to continue the unhealthy pace. He could devote ninety per cent of his energy into work and still have an orderly, well-maintained refuge to come home to because I kept it that way. He could maintain great relationships with the kids because I kept close track of them and warned him when one of them had a special need or was beginning to feel neglected. He could schedule back-to-back trips because I scrambled to get him ready to go again and covered all the bases while he was gone. I didn't want to do all those things, but I did them anyway.

It would have been better for me and for him if I had quit caretaking years ago – or better yet, had never started. I wouldn't have gotten lost along the way, and perhaps Bill wouldn't have pushed himself until he crashed.

You Can't Love what Isn't There

Some people get lost along the way because they have low self-esteem. Others end up with low self-esteem because they get lost along the way. For years they treat others as if they are more important than themselves, and eventually they begin to believe it.

L

I have long been aware of my sagging self-esteem. But I couldn't understand where it came from. I grew up in a loving, warm, supportive family. My parents are still the two biggest cheerleaders in my life. They always told me I could do anything or be anything or accomplish anything I wished. As a teenager and young adult I was positive and cheerful and happy.

So why, I often wondered, *do I feel like such a failure now? Why do I dislike myself so much?*

I realize now that throughout my adult years I gave so much of myself away that eventually there was little left for me to feel good about. There was little left to love.

It wasn't just because I was taking too much responsibility for Bill's life. I was busy trying to please everyone else, too. That often happens to Christian leaders. They know people are looking at them and they don't want to offend anybody, so they play it safe. They watch how they dress and what they drive. They watch what they say and to whom they say it. They watch how they spend their time and where they spend their money. They do their best to respond to everyone's requests and satisfy everyone's demands. Pretty soon, they become little more than a reflection of others' expectations. They don't know what they want any more – or who they are. They have lost their individuality, and they don't like what is left.

You Can't Hug Air

Nobody wins when someone gets lost along the way.

The 'lost' person loses. He or she ends up feeling like a victim and enduring an unhappy existence.

God loses, even if the person got lost 'for His sake', because we can only really give ourselves to God if we have a self to give. We can only serve Him wholeheartedly if we serve Him joyfully. We can only love Him sincerely if we love Him out of peace-filled, grateful hearts. If we are unhappy with our lives we will probably be unhappy with

God. If we feel like victims, we will probably, on some level, blame Him.

And spouses lose too, even if they were beneficiaries of heroic caretaking or if they were rescued time and time again. They lose because they end up married to an empty person. They end up loving a mirage. And it's hard to love a mirage. You can't hug air.

Loving doesn't mean we submerge our personhood in someone else's. Making a marriage work doesn't mean we have to give up who we are. The goal of a healthy marriage is for both spouses to maintain their individuality and bring their unique and valuable contributions to the relationship. We fell short of that goal and we both paid. But no more.

L

I have been very open with Todd and Shauna about the journey I have been on recently. When they want to encourage me along the path they say, 'Get a life, Mum. Get a life!'

That's what I'm doing.

I have dramatically reduced the pace of my life by learning to say no. I am asking Bill for more help on the home front and receiving an enthusiastic, willing response. I am travelling less and liking it more. I have crawled out from under unreasonable relational expectations and narrowed my circle of close friends. I am 'treating myself', to nature – walking forest preserve trails, driving down country roads, photographing wildflowers – just because I enjoy it. I am spending more time with my extended family. I am making time to write.

And I am loving it! I am experiencing a level of happiness that I haven't known in years. My stomach ache disappeared and I am sleeping better. I feel productive and fulfilled. I am having a great time with my kids. My relationship with God is more authentic than it has ever been.

And my marriage? Let me just say that the only person happier about these changes than I am is Bill.

Reaping the Rewards

Crisis mode living and unhealthy caretaking took a toll on our marriage for years. We worked hard in many areas and made a lot of progress. But all the while a subterranean stream of tension and hurt meandered deep down in the loamy soil of our relationship. We look back and think, *If only we had known. If only we had understood what we were doing. If only we had made changes sooner.*

But we also look forward. And when we do, we nearly burst with hope. We feel as if we are entering a new era. We've paid the price of self-discovery; now we get to reap the rewards. We know we will still sin, and sometimes hurt one another, and vacillate between extremes. But in a very dramatic way, we are different people now than we were before. We are both living more consistently with how God made us. We have acknowledged our Achilles' heels and our unhealthy behaviours, and we have made changes. We are happier, healthier individuals, and that frees us to be more loving spouses.

This morning we sat in a sunlit coffee shop and thanked one another for growing, for working, and for enduring. We both know a lot about enduring. Enduring means refusing to give up in the middle of a crisis, and being humble enough to ask for help. It means trudging along when you don't see the light at the end of the tunnel, and holding on when you don't want to. In the few remaining pages of this book we want to highlight a few specific principles that helped us endure during difficult days.

Notes

1. Melody Beattie, *Codependent No More* (San Francisco: Harper & Row Publishers, 1987), p. 78.
2. Beattie, *Codependent*, p. 79.
3. Beattie, *Codependent*, p. 84.

4. Beattie, *Codependent*, p. 87.
5. Beattie, *Codependent*, p. 86.
6. Dr Henry Cloud, *When Your World Makes No Sense* (Nashville: Thomas Nelson Publishers, 1990), p. 105.
7. Beattie, *Codependent*, p. 81.
8. Beattie, *Codependent*, p. 80.
9. Cloud, *When Your World Makes No Sense*, p. 177.
10. Beattie, *Codependent*, p. 198.

Staying Together When Life Is Tearing You Apart

Few marriages as difficult as ours survive. In fact, the closer we look at our marriage, the more amazed we are that it has survived. Love and respect had drawn us to one another, and on 18 May 1974, we joined hands and vowed to walk through life together. But before we celebrated our first anniversary, our different family backgrounds and temperaments had begun to pull us apart. Poor conflict resolution skills further strained our clutching hands. We held on for dear life, but when the romance in our marriage began to die, we nearly lost our grip. Crisis mode living and unhealthy caretaking made it even harder to hold on. We choked on the bile of hidden hostilities and didn't want to hold on. We reached painful impasses, and wondered if it was worth holding on.

But we held on. We stayed together when life was tearing us apart, and we ended up with a solid, healthy marriage that is getting better every day.

But why have we managed to hold on when so many people haven't? Was it raw strength? Willpower? Did we know how to grit out teeth better than the rest? Or were there other factors that gave us an edge and kept us from giving up too soon? During a recent Thursday morning breakfast date, we asked each other those questions. We want to end this book with our answers.

A Life-changing Difference

The first answer is that what helped us hold on more than anything else was that we maintained spiritual authenticity. We looked for truth and guidance in the Bible. We memorized verses that encouraged us to be kind, loving, honest, and patient. We prayed for help. We begged God to give us insight and understanding and creative ideas. We asked ourselves again and again, 'What does God want us to do now? How would Jesus handle this situation? What attitude would He have? What words would He say?' We tried our best to obey God, and when we failed to, we repented. Many times we didn't want to do those things. Sometimes, in fact, we both wished we weren't Christians. We wished that pleasing God didn't matter to us. We wished we could be hard-hearted without feeling bad about it. We wished we could slam doors without regretting it. And turn our backs on our spouses without hearing a divine whisper: *Don't do that. You'll be sorry. You have too much to lose.* Sometimes we would have given anything not to have to do the right thing.

But submitting ourselves to God, even as halfheartedly and unhappily as we sometimes did, kept our hearts soft. It didn't make us perfect – far from it – but it made us flexible and humble. It kept us on the right track. It kept us working at marriage.

If your Christianity is merely a matter of talk, we challenge you to take it further. Let it change your life. Study the Bible. Pray. Obey God. See what a difference it can make in your marriage.

If you aren't a Christian, please examine the truths of Christianity with an open mind. Jesus Christ died to free all of us from the tyranny of sin and to reconcile us to God and to one another.

If you are a Christian, but your spouse isn't, please make your continued spiritual growth a priority. You cannot change your spouse, but you can change yourself. You can tap God's power to a greater degree, and become stronger and more loving and more mature. Then you can pray earnestly that your spouse will one day choose to submit to the God you have submitted to.

What Can We Learn?

We also agreed that taking advantage of the wonderful self-help resources available today greatly increased our holding power. We went to seminars and workshops and conferences on marriage. We listened to tapes on marriage. We read books on marriage.

Oh, did we read books! We read together and read separately. We read on vacation and read ourselves to sleep at night. We read books by theologians and psychologists and marriage counsellors. We read about temperaments, personal growth, workaholism, conflict resolution, sex, stress management, how to relax, how to raise kids, how to handle money. We latched on to every good idea we could find, and it helped tremendously.

Some people give up before they read the first book, or listen to the first tape, or attend the first workshop. That's a tragedy. Only we are to blame if we fail to use the incredible resources at our disposal.

We also benefited from being in a church that put strong emphasis on marriage and family life. If your church doesn't provide challenging, insightful, practical teaching that helps you become a better spouse, perhaps another church could serve you better.

Hold Us Accountable

One of the wisest choices we made was to open our marriage to the scrutiny of close friends. We have always had someone, usually a couple, with whom we could discuss the truth about our relationship, with whom we could say, 'We had a terrible fight last night and we're hurting.' Or, 'We are stuck and we need help.' Or, 'We are discouraged. We've been working so hard and getting nowhere.'

Sometimes we just needed a safe place to blow off steam so we could settle down and talk constructively. At other times we needed advice from people who knew and loved both of us. We often needed somebody to cheer us on, to root for us, to say, 'We love you two, and we know you can make it through this. We have so much invested in this marriage. Keep trying. It'll be worth it.'

Coming to grips with crisis mode living and unhealthy caretaking were the greatest breakthroughs of our adult lives. We are very thankful for the loving couple who went on the sometimes painful, sometimes exhilarating journey with us. Many times we needed the perspective of outside observers. Often they helped us sort through our jumble of tangled insights and put our thoughts into words. They rejoiced when we made progress, and grieved when we didn't. They took care of our kids when we needed time alone. They sat through silly movies when we needed to laugh. They held us accountable when they saw us slipping.

'How's your schedule, Bill? Are you keeping it under control?'

'Are you taking care of yourself, Lynne? Are you being honest about what you need?'

Most people in past generations were hesitant to be vulnerable, particularly in regard to marriage. 'We're doing just fine,' they'd say. 'Just fine.' We chose the opposite approach: to be open, to invite a few trustworthy, proven friends inside our relationship. We think it was a wise choice and encourage you to do the same.

If you and your spouse are not close to another couple, we challenge you to begin now to build such a friendship.

You could join a couples' group at your church or invite some couples over for dinner. When you discover a husband and wife you both enjoy spending time with, meet with them again. If the four of you continue to 'click', you have a foundation to build on. If you don't, you can try someone else. You won't build a solid couples' friendship overnight; it will take an investment of time and effort. But it may be one of the best things you ever do for your marriage.

Remember When…

Identifying a few activities that minimized our differences and provided a respite from our struggles also helped us hold on. We discovered, for example, that we enjoy driving long distances together. As different as we are, when we cloister ourselves within the confines of a car, we seem to mesh easily. Maybe it's because we are forced to travel at the same pace. Maybe it's because we are isolated from outside pressures. Whatever the reason, we both become unusually easygoing and lighthearted, our conversations ambling pleasantly off on interesting side roads and unexpected detours. We both enjoy winding our way through rural towns and eating lunch in down-home diners. We always feel that we're a mile or two ahead of responsibility and just out of reach of real life.

Sailing does the same for us, to an even greater degree. We don't own a boat, but gracious friends often let us use theirs. We always have a wonderful time. We trim the sails, set our course, and feel like we are in paradise. Shortly after one particularly enjoyable trip, we entered one of the roughest eras of our marriage. We both felt like giving up, but we kept remembering how well we had gotten along on the sailing ship. We kept remembering the laughter and the romance, and that memory propelled us into the future. Reminding ourselves of the happiness we had known then motivated us to recapture it.

Holidays, getaways, recreation and fun sometimes make the difference between letting go and hanging on. Creating pleasant memories doesn't have to cost a lot of money, but the result can be priceless.

Painful Realities

Ministers and their spouses hear more than a normal share of sad stories. People pour out their hearts in phone calls and letters and counselling sessions. As grieved as we have been by these accumulated tragedies, hearing them has helped us by giving us a glimpse of reality.

Some people imagine divorce as an easy way out, but we learned through other people's experiences that husbands, wives, and children all pay a heavy price when marriages fail. People who opt for divorce unwittingly trade one set of problems for another, and the postdivorce problems are often far harder to resolve than the marital problems would have been. A divorce lawyer told us that most couples he deals with say they wish they had worked to build their marriages as hard as they have to work to survive divorce.

Working through a difficult marriage may be painful, but usually not as painful as giving up. Each time we got weary of the work, we thought of the stories we had heard and the devastation we had seen, and we found strength to hold on a little longer.

How to Cry for Help

Problems, conflicts, and differences can lead to divorce court, but they don't have to if couples learn how to seek constructive help.

A woman we know who committed adultery said, 'I was miserable, and I didn't think I had any options. I didn't know how to cry for help. Finally, I couldn't stand it any more ... so I did something stupid.' Because she was a leader in her church, she was afraid to admit to her friends how troubled her marriage was. She was also afraid of the stigma of going to a counsellor. So she did nothing, until she couldn't hold on any longer, and she sought help in another man's bed.

Instead of getting so desperate that we committed adultery, or ran away, or did some other destructive thing, we found legitimate ways to cry for help. We poured out our frustrations to God and sought His help. We were honest with each other about how desperate we sometimes felt, even saying difficult things like, 'I'm drifting away from you. I'm being tempted by other people. We need to do something about this.' We picked up the books again. We talked to friends. Again, watching other people travel the downward spiral all the way to the bottom made us determined to do *whatever we had to do* to avoid descending into desperation.

For many couples, professional counselling may be the best way to cry for help. It grieves us that so many people in faltering marriages hesitate to seek counsel. We firmly believe that many estranged couples could have avoided appointments with the divorce lawyer had they scheduled appointments with a marriage counsellor soon enough.

A temporary separation may be helpful for other couples. We suggest separation not as an alternative to marriage, but as an alternative to divorce. We have known husbands and wives who were so frustrated and hurt by marital conflicts that they truly wanted out of their marriages. However, after a period of separation under the guidance of a wise counsellor, they were able to reconcile with their spouse and rebuild their relationship. A time of individual healing often enables spouses to face the challenge of marriage later, with renewed energy and wisdom.

A separation is probably necessary if there is any form of physical abuse taking place in a marriage, and often advisable when there is substance abuse involved. Scripture repeatedly affirms the sanctity and permanence of marriage, and this book is dedicated to helping married people stay together. But the Bible also eloquently proclaims the worth of the individual, denounces violence, and calls for Christians to respond with compassion and kindness to those who have been oppressed or harmed or taken advantage of. It is in that spirit of Christian compassion that we encourage spouses in abusive situations to temporarily get out and to cry for help as loudly as they can.

Call it Commitment

For us, the final key to holding on was learning not to panic every time we hit a crisis.

When we are getting along well we say we are *connecting*. When we are connected we love being together, we talk easily and laugh freely, we touch each other naturally and lovingly, we encourage each other, we celebrate each other's uniqueness, we serve each other joyfully, and we tease each other playfully. Connection is the goal of marriage; it is the oneness the Bible talks about. It's wonderful, it's happy, and it's fun.

But we discovered long ago that it takes precious little for us to *disconnect*. Sin, temperament differences, exhaustion, outside pressures, the demands of life – any one or all of these can push us into a way of relating that is anything but wonderful and happy and fun.

Early in our marriage, whenever we disconnected, we panicked. We thought any slip from perfect oneness signalled disaster. We were on the ropes. Divorce was inevitable. We might as well tag the furniture and divvy up the silverware. There was no hope and no turning back. We felt like we were caught in an angry current, destined for a deadly crash on a rocky reef. We always managed to avoid the crash – just in the nick of time – but that didn't lessen our fear of disconnection.

Then one night, during a sensitive discussion of our then-current disconnection, we realized that because we both meant our wedding vows, had a spirit of reconciliation, and were willing to plough through the work of conflict resolution, we did not have to panic over disconnection. We did not have to assume we were headed for ruin. We could untag the furniture and put away the silver. We weren't going anywhere. We were *committed* to one another.

That made a tremendous difference to us. We quit thinking of disconnection as a precursor of disaster, and quit predicting gloom and doom. We began to call disconnection the 'commitment phase'. Instead of focusing on the negative, we reminded one another of the positive: in spite of the difficulty we were facing, we had a rock-solid commitment to one another that would see us through disconnection and back into oneness.

Being imperfect people in an imperfect marriage, we are going to disconnect periodically. And living in a busy world means that we can't always rush right out for a three-hour dinner to figure out what went wrong. Sometimes it may be two or three days before we can fully address the real issues. That is when the commitment phase serves us well. During those awkward hours of waiting we keep reminding ourselves of our mutual commitment. Yes, there is a problem. Yes, it might be serious. But we don't have to slide to the edge of ruin because of it. We're not going to do anything destructive or stupid. We are going to pray fervently for one another, we are going to treat each other respectfully and courteously, and we are going to work our way back to connection.

The commitment phase is not the goal of marriage or what courting couples dream about. It doesn't hold a candle to romance. But it is a far better alternative than despair.

It is, in essence, an affirmation of hope. It is a noble, valiant refusal to give up. It is a wide-angle view of life, a disciplined willingness to fix our sights beyond the problem at hand and focus on the reality of future reconnection.

When we were twenty-two, love and unbridled optimism convinced us that we were more than ready to become ideal spouses. We were, or so we believed, fit to be tied.* By thirty-two, we had been initiated into reality many times over. Fights and frustrations had led to anguish and anger. We had had it. We *were* fit to be tied.

Now we stand on the edge of another decade. We are less idealistic than we were at twenty-two, but far happier than we were at thirty-two. We have fought battles and jumped hurdles and learned lessons and held on. And now we can say confidently what we said naively years ago: we really *are* fit to be tied.

---

* 'Fit to be tied' is also a colloquial expression, often used in America, meaning 'angry enough to burst'.